The Bluebell Railway

Five Decades of Achievement

MICHAEL WELCH

Capital Transport

in association with The Bluebell Railway

ISBN 978-1-85414-336-5

Published by
Capital Transport Publishing
www.capitaltransport.com

Printed by
1010 Printing International

© Michael Welch 2010

Front cover: Bluebell steam personified. LBSCR E4 Class No.32473 takes the 4.55pm Kingscote to Horsted Keynes train past the site of Ingwersen's nursery, about a mile south of Kingscote, on 21st April 2007. This is a short working which terminated at Horsted Keynes, where passengers for Sheffield Park were obliged to change – just like a real train journey! *Graham Mallinson*

Title page: One of the unofficial perks of being a working member on the Bluebell Railway is the ability to obtain pictures from unusual positions out of bounds to ordinary members of the public. In this shot, taken from the top of Horsted Keynes' down starting signal, a triple-headed train waits to depart from Platforms 4/5 in August 2004. The stock and train engine had formed the 4.47pm *ex*-Sheffield Park, while locomotives *Birch Grove* and *Fenchurch*, which had earlier been used on a 'Fenchurch Special', had been attached to the front of the train after bringing empty coaching stock up from Sheffield Park. Note all three engines face southwards. In the background a connecting train from Kingscote can just be discerned. *Ian Wright*

Back cover: The Bluebell Railway is fortunate enough to possess some of the finest preserved stations in Great Britain which conjure up the atmosphere of branch line rail travel in a bygone age. Sheffield Park station is famous for its display of enamel advertisements, Horsted Keynes for the track with platforms on both sides while Kingscote offers passengers peace and solitude. These two pictures were taken at Sheffield Park station. *Chris Gammell/Bluebell archive* and *John Scrace*

Introduction

During the afternoon of 17th May 1960 former LBSCR 'Terrier' locomotive No.55 (later *Stepney*) left Brighton with two coaches in tow, bound for Horsted Keynes and a new home at the fledgling Bluebell Railway. Voluntary railway preservation at that time was confined to a few Welsh narrow gauge lines and the goods-only Middleton Railway at Leeds, so the concept of operating a passenger service on a standard gauge line was a leap into the unknown. Prophets of doom abounded but they had not reckoned with the persistence and sheer determination of the founders, nor their wonderful flair for publicity, because when No.55 steamed into Horsted Keynes station it was greeted not only by an enthusiastic group of Bluebell members but also press representatives and television camera crews. The train's arrival marked not only the start of the Bluebell venture but also, arguably, the start of voluntary standard gauge railway preservation in Great Britain.

During the ensuing weeks another locomotive was obtained from BR, a locomotive shed was built at Sheffield Park station, where the Bluebell had set up its headquarters and tickets were printed, together with a host of other vital jobs. Before any public train could operate the preservationists had to obtain a Light Railway Order from the Ministry of Transport which involved a thorough inspection to verify the Bluebell Railway's ability to operate the line safely. This took place on 9th July 1960, the Railway passing with flying colours, and the grand opening day was set for 7th August. The pessimists had suffered the first of many defeats! When the opening day came there were unprecedented scenes at Sheffield Park station, with around 2,000 people thronging the platforms and it is estimated that 900 passengers were carried as far as the newly-constructed Bluebell Halt, just south of Horsted Keynes. It was clear that the idea of a steam-operated line run by enthusiasts had caught the imagination of the general public and the Bluebell's success continued during the rest of the summer. When the line closed at the end of October more than 15,000 passengers had been carried, a figure beyond the most optimistic predictions. It is fair to say that after such a splendid start the Bluebell has never looked back!

The elegance of Victorian engineering. A close-up shot of the Adams 'Radial' tank locomotive. *Chris Gammell / Bluebell archive*

This book charts the development and growth of the Bluebell Railway from the pioneering line of August 1960, run by amateurs, to the world-renowned major tourist attraction it is today. I have attempted to chronicle all of the major events and landmarks in the Railway's history but, inevitably, it has not been possible to cover everything within the space available, and I can only express the hope that the illustrations that follow are a reasonably balanced selection that portray the highlights of fifty years of progress. What does the future hold for the Bluebell? It is likely that by the time this book is available work on Operation Undercover will be well underway and the large storage shed for coaching stock, desperately needed to protect the Bluebell's priceless collection of wooden-bodied carriages, will be taking shape. Then in a couple of years or so there is the absolutely mouth watering prospect of the new-build LBSCR Atlantic *Beachy Head* steaming out of Sheffield Park. The long-cherished dream of reaching East Grinstead, one of the railway's major objectives for many years, is yet to be realised (at the time of writing) and there are daunting financial hurdles to be faced, but the railway has faced formidable challenges in the past and successfully overcome them. There is every reason to believe that the next fifty years will be just as eventful as the last!

I have been very fortunate to have had the help of many Bluebell colleagues and others who kindly supplied pictures for publication and, undoubtedly, without their willing assistance compilation of this album would not have been possible. In addition, John Beckett, Chris Cooper, Chris Evans, Dave Fakes, Roger Williams and Ian Wright have checked the manuscript, made many constructive criticisms and suggested worthwhile improvements, for which I am most grateful. I would particularly like to thank Graham Mallinson, a life-long Bluebell member, who has been unfailingly helpful during the compilation of this book and provided much additional information on a variety of topics. I accept full responsibility for any errors that have remained undetected.

Michael Welch

The decorative and colourful SECR crest on H Class 0-4-4T No.263. *Chris Gammell / Bluebell archive*

Contents

1960–1969

Start of public passenger service

Acquisition of LSWR Adams 'Radial' locomotive

Visit of Caledonian Railway 'Single' No.123

Purchase of freehold of Sheffield Park to Horsted Keynes line

1970–1979

Construction of carriage shed at Horsted Keynes

Work starts on new locomotive works at Sheffield Park

Bulleid Pacific No.21C123 *Blackmore Vale* enters traffic

Influx of locomotives from Barry scrap yard

1980–1989

Centenary of Lewes to East Grinstead line commemorated

Secretary of State for Transport gives go ahead for East Grinstead extension

Construction of buffet building at Sheffield Park

First section of track laid north of Horsted Keynes

1990–1999

Extension shuttle from Horsted Keynes to Horsted House farm inaugurated

Kingscote station becomes northern terminus of the line

First restored Metropolitan Railway coaches enter service

Filming of 'The Railway Children'

2000–2009

New carriage workshop completed

Last pieces of land purchased for Northern Extension

Royal visit by Princess Alexandra

Agreement reached on Woodpax site purchase

1960 The Bluebell's first items of rolling stock, former London Brighton & South Coast Railway (LBSCR) A1X Class 0-6-0T No.55 and two coaches, arrived on 17th May 1960; these were followed on 27th June by former South Eastern & Chatham Railway (SE&CR) P Class 0-6-0T No.323. The latter locomotive was certainly not the first choice of the majority of members, who would have much preferred another A1X Class engine (universally known to enthusiasts as 'Terriers'), but these were still required by British Railways for traffic purposes, principally on the Havant to Hayling Island branch, and consequently BR declined the Bluebell's request for another A1X Class locomotive. In the event the P Class proved to be very successful on the Bluebell and ideally suited to working the light trains that predominated during the early years. In this picture, taken on 2nd July 1960, the Railway's first locomotives can be seen in the original locomotive shed which was in the course of construction: the A1X Class engine is nearer to the camera. It should, perhaps, be mentioned that the *very first* locomotive to appear after the Bluebell's takeover was actually the Narrow Gauge Railway Society's diminutive 3ft 2¼in gauge 0-4-0T No.4 *Townsend Hook,* a Fletcher Jennings product of 1880 vintage, which arrived on 8th April 1960. *R.C. Riley*

Before the Bluebell could carry ordinary fare-paying passengers a detailed inspection had to be undertaken by the Ministry of Transport to ascertain whether the railway complied with stringent safety requirements. This exhaustive inspection by Col. J.H.R. Robertson took place on 9th July 1960, a Light Railway Order permitting the Society to operate the line being granted on 27th July, and it was decided to officially open the line to the public on 7th August. In addition to ensuring that statutory safety standards were met Society members were engaged in feverish 'behind the scenes' activity to ensure that the opening went according to plan. This involved organising refreshments for the general public, printing tickets and timetables and setting up a bookstall for the sale of souvenirs and suchlike. It was agreed that the Bluebell's coaches would be repainted in blue livery, in striking contrast to the familiar BR green, and in this shot a member can be seen apparently applying undercoat to former London & South Western Railway (LSWR) third class vehicle No.S320 at Sheffield Park station, also on 2nd July 1960. The other coach, No.S6575, is a Maunsell-designed brake composite carriage dating from 1929. *R.C. Riley*

Various events in railway history, such as *Mallard*'s world speed record in 1938 and the nationalisation of the 'Big Four' ten years later stand out, but for Bluebell supporters and well-wishers the day they will always remember is Sunday 7th August 1960 when the line carried its first fare-paying passengers. Extensive publicity in the national and local media prior to the reopening day, not to mention gloriously fine weather, ensured that the platforms at Sheffield Park station were packed to capacity. The opening ceremony took place on the front running plate of SECR P Class 0-6-0T No.323, from which the Bluebell Railway Preservation Society's (BRPS) chairman, John Leroy, introduced the guests of honour, playwright Captain Anthony Kimmins and his wife. Following Captain Kimmins's brief speech Mrs Kimmins named No.323 *Bluebell* in the usual manner. This photograph appears to have been taken during the opening ceremony. Note the crowd of people on the track between the platforms, the locomotive's white coal and the gentleman standing, rather precariously, on the newly-repainted down platform canopy. *Les Dench*

When the speeches and christening of *Bluebell* were over, Captain Kimmins walked to the signal frame and, supervised by a Bluebell signalman, pulled off the up starting signal prior to the departure of the Bluebell's first public passenger train. He then joined the train, which was packed with invited guests and members of the press, and once *Bluebell* was coupled up at the other end of the two-coach formation the Bluebell Railway's first public passenger service, with No.55 *Stepney* at its head, was on its way to Horsted Keynes (Bluebell Halt). This remarkable achievement was the culmination of months of meticulous planning by dozens of hard-working Bluebell volunteers. It should be noted that, due to the lack of run-round facilities at Horsted Keynes, the Ministry of Transport had stipulated that a locomotive would be required at each end of the train. Here *Stepney* is seen awaiting departure with the first train as dozens of admiring bystanders line both platforms. What a wonderful occasion! *Les Dench*

Bluebell simmers in the down platform at Sheffield Park after returning on the first passenger train. The first train was scheduled to depart at 2.30pm and following workings were supposed to run at 50 minute intervals commencing at 3.45pm, but, in the event, due to the sheer number of intending passengers, it appears that the timetable was largely abandoned and trains continued to run into the evening, thus ensuring that everybody who wished to travel had taken a ride to Bluebell Halt and back; it must have been a very long and tiring day for the Bluebell staff involved. Perhaps it should be mentioned that Bluebell Halt was located just south of Horsted Keynes station and at that time was the railway's northern terminus. Right from the reopening day the Bluebell caught the imagination of the general public and it would be something of an understatement to say that the day was a resounding success beyond the Society's wildest expectations. Could the Bluebell have got off to a more promising start? *Les Dench*

Musical entertainment on the reopening day was provided by The Temperance Seven who were positioned at the north end of the up platform. In this picture a section of the band can be seen attracting a good deal of interest. A total of around 2,000 people are thought to have attended the reopening ceremony of whom around 900 were carried on the train, so it is no wonder the timetable had to be amended to accommodate them all! The Bluebell continued to operate at weekends only until the end of October, when it closed for the winter period, and patronage exceeded all expectations with a total of 15,000 passengers being carried. Among many prominent people who visited the line during this period were the Prime Minister, the Rt Hon Harold Macmillan and his wife, Lady Dorothy Macmillan. *Les Dench*

1961 The main event on the first day of the 1961 season was the naming of newly-arrived P Class 0-6-0T engine No.27 and this was carried out in the traditional manner by the Society's President, Bishop Geoffrey Warde, who pronounced 'I name this engine *Primrose.* May God bless those who drive and serve her and all who travel on the Bluebell Line this season'. The teams who painted *Stepney* and restored the museum received a special word of praise. The first train of the 1961 season left at 2.48pm with *Stepney* and *Primrose* at the front and *Bluebell* at the rear. This picture appears to show the opening train of the new season waiting in the up platform with *Bluebell* in the down platform prior to positioning itself at the rear of the train. Vintage London & South Western Railway coach No.S320 is also in the shot. *R.C. Riley*

Acquisition of an Adams 'Radial' tank locomotive had been one of the society's priorities from the very early days and this was achieved when No.488 (formerly BR No.30583) arrived from Eastleigh on 12th July 1961. It is depicted at Sheffield Park on 29th July. Three of these exceedingly graceful and well-proportioned locomotives had survived on the tightly-curved Axminster to Lyme Regis line to which they were ideally suited owing to their very short coupled wheelbase. They had defied all attempts to replace them until the branch was partially relaid in the early 1960s, thus permitting the veterans to be withdrawn. The class was introduced by the LSWR in 1882 for use on suburban services from Waterloo station and No.488 was constructed by Neilson & Co. of Glasgow in 1885. The locomotives started to be displaced as early as 1915 and No.488 was purchased by the government in 1916 which in turn sold it to the East Kent Railway in 1919. The Southern Railway acquired it in 1946 to relieve pressure on two sister engines employed on the Lyme Regis branch. The coaches, which were built for the Metropolitan Railway in 1898/1900, were 'surplus to requirements' following their displacement from the Chesham branch and were purchased from London Transport for a very reasonable sum. They arrived at Sheffield Park on 2nd March 1961 and provided a much-needed increase in seating capacity on Bluebell trains. *R.C. Riley*

In September 1961 it was announced that BR had provisionally agreed that the Bluebell Railway could operate into Horsted Keynes station from the start of the next season, subject to the completion of the necessary legal formalities. It was also agreed that, as a forerunner, Bluebell trains could work into the station with a BR pilotman on 29th October, the last day of the 1961 season. The running into Horsted Keynes main station would be a more convenient arrangement for people holding BR through excursion tickets and, the Bluebell management hoped, would also stimulate traffic on the branch from Haywards Heath which was threatened with closure. History was made, therefore, when the 1.48pm train from Sheffield Park steamed triumphantly into Horsted Keynes and the Bluebell became the first privately preserved line to operate over BR tracks. The train was hauled by *Stepney* piloting the Adams 'Radial' tank locomotive with the two SECR P Class engines on the rear. This historic event rounded off a very busy season with more than 70,000 passengers carried, including 15,000 during a highly successful sixteen days continuous running period in August. In this wonderful panoramic illustration, which was taken from the top of the erstwhile water tank, No.323 *Bluebell* can be seen 'blowing off' in Horsted Keynes station on 29th October 1961. *R.C. Riley*

1962 The 1962 season got off to a flying start with the visit of Great Northern Railway 0-6-0ST No.1247, the first steam locomotive bought for private operational preservation, which powered a special train named the 'Blue Belle' from London Bridge to Sheffield Park and return on 1st April. The train reversed at Haywards Heath before continuing to Horsted Keynes where *Stepney* was attached to the south end for the short run down to Sheffield Park. The eyebrows of many members were raised when the late Doctor Richard (later Lord) Beeching, who was busily engaged in 'reshaping' the BR network at that time, was invited along as the Bluebell's special guest. He opened the newly-constructed halt at Holywell and apparently gave the railway preservation movement, and the Bluebell in particular, his blessing. Another guest on the same day was Mr. George Weeden, Line Traffic Manager of the Southern Region's Central Section, without whose support the special train would probably not have operated. In this picture a gleaming No.1247 is seen on the right as *Bluebell* shunts the Metropolitan Railway 'Chesham' set at the south end of Sheffield Park station. On the return journey to London No.1247 proved to be a sprightly performer, reaching London Bridge four minutes early. The special was routed along the Quarry Line (avoiding Redhill) while the 'Brighton Belle' was reportedly relegated to travel via Coulsdon South! *R.C. Riley*

A general view of Sheffield Park station and yard taken in April 1962, looking northwards. No.323 *Bluebell* can be seen on the left while in the middle of the picture a small locomotive can just be discerned. This is the narrow gauge 0-4-0T No.4 *Townsend Hook* which, as previously mentioned, came to the line in April 1960 and was the first locomotive to arrive under the Bluebell's jurisdiction. Two newly delivered engines are visible on the right, the GWR 'Dukedog' 4-4-0 and the North London Railway 0-6-0T locomotive, both of which arrived in early 1962. One wonders what engines were hidden from view in the locomotive shed! *Alan Reeve*

On 21st October 1962 the Bluebell organised another rail tour from London to Sheffield Park, this time starting from Victoria and using preserved LSWR T9 Class 4-4-0 No.120 on the main line stretches with Bluebell Railway motive power from Haywards Heath to Sheffield Park and back. It is sad to think that just over a year later the vital Haywards Heath to Horsted Keynes branch was closed, thus putting an end to these jolly days out for Bluebell members. In this picture *Stepney*, in double harness with the Adams 'Radial' tank locomotive which had been restored to LSWR livery, is seen hastening along the Ardingly branch in the glorious autumn sunshine. By this time the Ardingly branch had been reduced to a single track for economy reasons, but the former down line, in the foreground, had remained *in situ* for the storage of rolling stock. *John Beckett*

The Bluebell's historic collection of locomotives was further enhanced when former LBSCR E4 Class 0-6-2T No.32473 was acquired from the Southern Region after withdrawal from traffic following its displacement from empty carriage workings between Waterloo and Clapham Junction. It was delivered on 16th October 1962 and apparently made its first public appearance on Bluebell metals five days later, hauling the rail tour from Victoria on the last stage of its journey from Horsted Keynes to Sheffield Park. Later that day it worked ordinary Bluebell services and in this picture is seen pausing at Holywell Halt in the afternoon sunshine with a train formed of the 'Chesham' set. At that time a large number of Bluebell members were devoted fans of the old LBSCR and would no doubt have greeted the arrival of the elegant E4 with great enthusiasm. Note that the first two digits of the engine's number and BR crest have been painted over. *R.C. Riley*

A number of Bluebell members considered that a halt should be provided at Holywell (Waterworks) adjacent to the road on which the Haywards Heath to Horsted Keynes bus service operated. They laboured throughout the winter of 1961/2 and the halt was formally opened (as previously mentioned) by Doctor Beeching on 1st April 1962. It was by far the most elaborate of the railway's halts, being equipped with a small shelter and it even had a tiny ticket office! Sadly, it failed to attract many bus passengers, but did catch the eye of passing motorists who parked on the narrow road thus creating considerable problems for other road users. This came to the notice of the local authority and the Bluebell came under pressure to move the halt's entrance to a more suitable location. This was not practicable, however, and the Bluebell management reluctantly decided to close the halt at the end of the 1962 season so all of the effort expended by members on building Holywell Halt was sadly wasted. From the commercial viewpoint its closure hardly affected the Railway, a derisory total of fifty tickets being issued during the entire 1962 season. In this rare shot of part of the structure *Primrose* is seen at the rear of a train to Sheffield Park, also on 21st October 1962. *R.C. Riley*

1963 The year 1962 was noteworthy for the influx of locomotives acquired for preservation, all welcome additions to the Bluebell fleet. In 1963, in complete contrast, there were no new arrivals but this lack of activity was more than compensated for by the running of various rail tours via the Ardingly branch. The 'Spring Belle' ran from Victoria to Sheffield Park on 31st March and employed BR Standard Class 4MT 2-6-4T No.80084, assisted by *Birch Grove* (as No.473 had been named), on the run down from London to Haywards Heath. On arrival there No.80084 continued to Brighton to turn, and later took the train back to London without assistance. Special permission had been given for the use of the E4 Class locomotive on BR metals. Undoubtedly, however, the highlight of the year for most members was the visit of the graceful Caledonian Railway 'Single' No.123 which, accompanied by restored LSWR T9 Class 4-4-0 No.120, powered the 'Scottish Belle' rail tour from Victoria to Haywards Heath and back on 15th September. No.123, which was built by Neilson & Co. of Glasgow in 1886, had a colourful career and took part in the 'Races to the North' in 1888 and was withdrawn from ordinary traffic in 1935. In 1958 the Scottish Region of British Railways had a flash of inspiration and restored it to full working order for use on special trains. One wonders, however, if they envisaged that the 'Single' would ever be used on specials as far away as Sussex! In this picture No.123 is seen standing at the north end of Horsted Keynes station after journeying from Brighton where it had been turned in readiness for the run back to London. After its journey back to Victoria No.123 was worked to Willesden shed later the same evening, the first port of call on its protracted journey home to Scotland. The train's official title was 'The Scottish Belle' but, rather confusingly, it carried 'The Blue Belle' headboard which appears to have been used on all Bluebell Railway tours in the very early 1960s regardless of their official title. *Rodney Lissenden*

The Bluebell management had high hopes that their BR connection at Horsted Keynes would boost passenger takings on the Ardingly branch and possibly save it from closure. Alas, it was not to be, and BR announced that the Haywards Heath to Horsted Keynes link, which was so invaluable to the Bluebell Railway, would close from 28th October 1963. The Bluebell decided to commemorate the demise of the Ardingly branch by running 'The Brighton Blue Belle' rail tour from Brighton to Sheffield Park and return with *Stepney* and *Birch Grove* as motive power on 27th October. The coaching stock used was an interesting selection of vintage vehicles normally employed on the Lancing carriage works staff train, commonly known as the 'Lancing Belle'. In this picture the train is seen crossing on to Bluebell metals north of Horsted Keynes station with *Bluebell* in charge, while apparently *Stepney* and *Birch Grove* are providing rear-end assistance. After euphoric scenes only six weeks previously when the Caledonian 'Single' visited Horsted Keynes, one can only imagine the sombre mood on this train with passengers mindful that the Bluebell was about to lose its vital passenger link with the 'outside world'. *R.C. Riley*

The train depicted in the previous shot is seen again with *Stepney* and *Birch Grove* prominent. Later that day the *very last* scheduled BR electric train departed from Horsted Keynes at 6.16pm and BR entered into the spirit of the occasion to some degree by providing 6-Pan unit No.3033, an unaccustomed sight on the Ardingly branch, to form the last working. This reportedly left on time with nearly fifty people on board – quite a load for an Ardingly branch train. The Bluebell special pulled out at 6.40pm with *Stepney* and *Birch Grove* running bunker first, and as the train started to move the 6.25pm from Sheffield Park, with the Adams 'Radial' and P Class No.27 in charge, hove into view and immediately all five engines (*Bluebell* was still in the station area after bringing in the special) started a prolonged fanfare on their whistles which reportedly lasted half a minute. The final train of all was the Bluebell special, so the story of the Haywards Heath to Horsted Keynes branch ended as it had began – with steam traction! But what a desperately sad occasion. The two Bluebell locomotives later returned to Sheffield Park after being coaled and watered at Brighton shed. *R.C. Riley*

1964 Many Bluebell members who were aficionados of the LBSCR had wanted the Railway to acquire another 'Terrier' (Class A1X) locomotive and, after a very long wait, in 1964 their wish was granted when further engines were made available by BR following closure of the Hayling Island branch in November 1963. The engine chosen was No.32636, formerly LBSCR No.72 *Fenchurch* which, by the time of its withdrawal, had reached the ripe old age of 91 years and was the oldest surviving engine in the BR fleet. In addition, a group of members had recently purchased a LBSCR milk van from Lancing carriage works and special dispensation was granted for No.32636 to propel this vehicle up the Ardingly branch without a brake van, a most unorthodox method of operation. This movement, the last along the branch before track lifting started, took place on 13th May 1964. The Bluebell were quick to renumber No.32636 (by the simple expedient of painting out the first digit) which is seen here standing in a somewhat deserted looking Horsted Keynes station on 23rd May 1964. *R.C. Riley*

The Great Western Railway 90XX Class, commonly known as the 'Dukedog' class, was introduced in 1936 using parts from much earlier designs and the Bluebell Railway's example, No.9017, was assembled at Swindon Works in 1938. The locomotive ended its days at Machynlleth shed in Wales in October 1960 and was the final surviving locomotive in BR service with outside frames. Following its withdrawal No.9017 was stored in the old Cambrian Railway's works at Oswestry while funds were raised to purchase the engine from BR for preservation. Thankfully, the preservation fund was successful and No.9017 arrived on Bluebell metals on 15th February 1962, the locomotive being routed via Brighton for turning purposes.

It was the first tender engine in the Bluebell fleet and must have seemed a very large machine indeed compared to other locomotives on the railway at that time. In this portrait No.9017 is seen on Freshfield bank in what could be termed a 'transitional' livery – it is still in BR black but carrying *Earl of Berkeley* nameplates. This picture was taken in October 1964, shortly before its restoration during the 1964/65 winter period to GWR livery as No.3217 which was its original number. The vehicle immediately behind the 'Dukedog' is a former London & North Western Railway Observation car which also ended its days in BR service in Wales, in this case on the scenic branch from Llandudno to Blaenau Ffestiniog. *Roy Hobbs*

Almost unrecognisable compared to today, this is a general view of Sheffield Park station in October 1964 with *Fenchurch* standing in the down platform at the head of the 'Chesham' set and observation car. Note the fashions of that period! *Ian Wright*

The year 1964 produced record receipts and there was no doubt that the Bluebell Railway had become established as a major tourist attraction. Whilst the future for the preserved section looked rosy, 1964 was also a very sad year, because in July track lifting between Ardingly and East Grinstead (except in the immediate area of Horsted Keynes) commenced and there was the grim realisation among members that the Bluebell was soon to become physically isolated from the BR system. The lifting gang's small diesel shunter broke down soon after work started and they hired a Bluebell locomotive as a replacement so the Railway at least benefited financially from the dismantling operation. A lot of salvaged material was sold to the National Coal Board while the conductor rails went to blast furnaces in South Wales. *Birch Grove* was used on the demolition trains for a short period but the lion's share of the work was undertaken by the North London tank locomotive No.2650. Here it is seen standing amidst piles of track panels at West Hoathly, where the contractors made their base, in December 1964. Who would have guessed that thirty years later the same engine would be used to relay the line north of Horsted Keynes? *Roy Hobbs*

1965

The two most notable events at the Bluebell in 1965 occurred within a few days of each other, namely the delivery of the LBSCR inspection saloon No.60 and celebrations to mark the fifth anniversary of Bluebell operations. The 63ft 8in long saloon is a magnificent twelve-wheeled vehicle constructed in 1913 at Lancing works for the use of the directors and principal officers of the LBSCR. It consists of two main saloons, the larger of which is 26ft long, separated by a small kitchen, pantry and lavatory compartment. The beautiful interior panelling features mahogany and satin-wood while the ceilings are especially decorative. In Southern Railway days the saloon was renumbered 291S and various structural alterations were undertaken, most notably the fitting of end gangways which radically changed the vehicle's appearance. The coach was usually kept under cover at Stewarts Lane depot and upon withdrawal in early 1965 it was considered for preservation by the Curator of Historic Relics but, as a result of changed circumstances, the Bluebell was offered the coach. An anonymous donor provided the purchase price while various members dipped into their pockets to raise the equally large sum needed to cover the road transport. It is seen here entering Sheffield Park yard during the course of delivery on 4th August 1965. When the coach arrived there was still a packet of corn flakes in the pantry! The saloon was used on scheduled service trains for some years but its condition deteriorated and in recent years it has languished out of use. Restoration will be a costly operation but, perhaps one day, a wealthy benefactor might come to the coach's rescue. *Rodney Lissenden*

The centrepiece of the fifth anniversary celebrations on 8th August was a re-enactment of the original train of 1960 and everything was reproduced down to the smallest detail with the identical rolling stock and train crews being used. What a pity *Stepney* had undergone a personality change in the meantime, having been repainted in LBSCR livery! Special guests included a member of parliament and various local dignitaries. Here, the 2.48pm special from Sheffield Park to Horsted Keynes awaits departure with a gleaming *Stepney* at the front of the train. In the early days of the Bluebell, staff were often attired in Victorian costume on special occasions, a custom that was extremely popular with the general public, and a colourful group of members adds interest to the scene. Later the same day the LBSCR inspection saloon made its inaugural run on the 4.00pm from Sheffield Park. *Les Dench*

1966 In this picture the North London tank locomotive, by this time restored as No.2650, rolls into Horsted Keynes with a train from Sheffield Park in April 1966. During the first few years of its existence the Bluebell had operated on the basis of a five-year lease amounting to £2,250 per annum which had been negotiated in December 1959, together with an option to purchase the line for £34,000 at any time during the continuance of the lease. In the meantime BR policy had hardened and they now preferred to sell property outright rather than grant leases, so when the Bluebell approached BR regarding purchasing the land in 1964 BR's response was to demand £65,000, a sum well beyond the railway's resources. A Line Purchase Fund was set up with the initial objective of raising £20,000 and the Bluebell entered a period of severe financial stringency during which time expenditure was cut to the bone. Perhaps mindful that it would be a public relations disaster for BR if it closed the Bluebell down, the lease was extended piecemeal and, after protracted negotiations, a figure of £43,500 was agreed upon in the late autumn of 1967. *Roy Hobbs*

Locomotive restoration the hard way! *Bluebell* operated in black livery from the opening of the line until mid-1965 when it was taken out of traffic for overhaul and repainting in the Bluebell Railway's own blue livery. This decision no doubt upset the purists but at least the new colour was attractive and distinctive, important factors when so much of the line's income comes from the general public, not railway enthusiasts. In this shot, *Bluebell* is seen being repainted in the open air, without any protection from the elements, and the volunteers carrying out the work were no doubt praying that their handiwork would not be ruined by a sudden squall of rain. It is amazing that the Railway's locomotive department was able to maintain its fleet in such primitive conditions. This picture was taken on 2nd July 1966 and *Bluebell* returned to service in September. *R.C. Riley*

1967 During the compilation of this album, which aimed to cover every year since the Bluebell opened, it immediately became apparent that very few colour pictures were taken on the line during certain years: one such year was 1967, for which only a few transparencies were submitted. This was the last full year of BR steam and it is likely that most railway photographers were preoccupied with the 'alternative attractions' being staged by BR, such as the end of steam on the Southern Region in July and the last summer of steam working over Shap summit, and the Settle to Carlisle line. In this illustration *Stepney* is seen rounding the curve at Freshfield with a couple of blue-liveried coaches in tow on a sunny 20th August 1967. *John Scrace*

Another rare picture from 1967! The diminutive A1X Class 'Terrier' No.72 *Fenchurch* is dwarfed by its surroundings at Horsted Keynes station on 2nd September as it awaits departure with the 'Wealden Rambler'. At that time the station was still looking somewhat neglected with overgrown bushes and large areas of weeds. *R.C. Riley*

1968

Whilst it could be argued that very little of interest took place on the Bluebell in 1968 on the rolling stock front, behind the scenes the year proved to be an absolutely crucial one in the history of the Bluebell Railway. On 27th October contracts were exchanged with BR for the purchase of the railway, this involving an immediate down payment of £23,500 (available as a result of the success of the Line Purchase Fund) with the balance of £20,000 payable over the ensuing five years. After periods of great anxiety, scrimping and saving plus seemingly never-ending appeals to members for money, the Bluebell's future was much clearer and the management could now start to plan ahead in the knowledge that the line was safe at last. During 1968 an anonymous benefactor offered to purchase a locomotive for the railway with the result that BR Standard Class 4MT 4-6-0 No.75027, which was out of service at Carnforth in Lancashire, was earmarked as the best available engine which was suitable for use on the Bluebell. This was a wonderful expression of confidence in the Railway's future but, even so, there were many who doubted the need for such a large locomotive. Here, a southbound train approaches Rock Cutting with No.473 *Birch Grove* in charge in the spring of 1968. *Charles Whetmath / Bluebell Archive*

A landmark at Horsted Keynes was the remarkably tall LBSCR up starting signal which dominates this overall view of the station. *Birch Grove* sits in the platform with a motley rake of coaches in various liveries. This scene was also recorded in the spring of 1968, when nature appeared to be taking over large areas of the station premises. *Charles Whetmath / Bluebell Archive*

1969 'Good heavens, what does the Bluebell want a monster like that for?', might well have been the reaction of many at the Bluebell, where most trains were still powered by 0-6-0T locomotives, to the arrival of BR Standard Class 4MT 4-6-0 No.75027. It later turned out that this engine merely represented the shape of things to come as the character of the Bluebell changed from a line generally operating small tank locomotives to one worked by much larger mixed traffic and express passenger engines. No.75027, a Swindon product built in 1954, had quite an eventful life on BR, working for a time on the legendary Somerset and Dorset line before being transferred to the north-west of England where it ended its career on BR. No.75027 gained a place in the history books when, in May 1968, it became the last banking engine at Oxenholme for assisting trains up Grayrigg bank in the Lake District. It arrived on Bluebell metals on 22nd January 1969 and made its debut in traffic six months later on 27th July. It was still in BR condition when this portrait was taken on 12th April 1969. Note the rather unsightly temporary shed extension in the background which provided a desperately needed additional covered working area. *Chris Gammell / Bluebell Archive*

Bluebell in its new guise. After running for many years in black No.323 was repainted in 'Bluebell blue' and re-entered service in this livery, as previously mentioned, in September 1966. It was fitted with cast number and nameplates which really enhanced its appearance. In this shot it is seen approaching Sheffield Park station on 12th April 1969 with a short train formed of a SECR 'Birdcage' brake coach and the LNWR observation car. *Chris Gammell / Bluebell Archive*

Many pictures have been taken over the years of trains climbing the 1 in 75 gradient into Horsted Keynes station but, for a change, here is one of a train descending the bank on 3rd August 1969. The leading engine is LBSCR A1X Class 0-6-0T No.72 *Fenchurch* which at the time of this picture had been repainted in the livery of the Newhaven Harbour Company. In 1898 No.72 became the first locomotive of its class to be sold when it was purchased for use at Newhaven. The train engine is SECR P Class 0-6-0T No.27 which formerly ran on the Bluebell in black livery named *Primrose*. Note Horsted Keynes' outer home signal on the left of the shot. This photograph was taken on 3rd August 1969. *David Clark*

1970

A train to Sheffield Park eases out of Horsted Keynes station behind No.473 *Birch Grove* on 19th April 1970. The second coach in the train is a former Caledonian Railway carriage which had been restored by BR for use on special trains north of the border. It arrived on the Bluebell in 1969 and, after a five years-long sojourn in Sussex, returned to its native Scotland in 1974 to be reunited with a sister vehicle preserved by the Scottish Railway Preservation Society. The coach just visible on the left of the photograph is one of the 'Chesham' set vehicles that had been repainted white for a film in 1967, but by this date the entire set was out of service. Horsted Keynes goods yard, on the right, which contained a number of coaches on the day this picture was taken, had been earmarked as the site of the Bluebell's new carriage shed. The railway's vintage wooden-bodied coaching stock fleet had been suffering badly from constant exposure to the elements and covered accommodation was desperately needed. The Tenth Anniversary Appeal was launched in 1970 to raise £7,000 for the erection of a four track carriage shed and construction commenced in January 1971, the first stock being moved into the shed two months later. At long last the Bluebell's priceless collection of historic vehicles had a roof over its head. *Chris Gammell / Bluebell Archive*

Photographers vie for the best position on the bridge at the north end of Sheffield Park station as No.3217 *Earl of Berkeley* pulls out with 'The Decadian' on 2nd August 1970. This train, as its name implies, was run to commemorate the Bluebell's tenth anniversary. This was the first occasion that relatively modern Bulleid-designed carriages (the second and third coaches in the formation) were used on the railway and they formed what might be loosely termed a 'main line set' with a couple of the railway's existing Maunsell vehicles. The Bulleid coaches had been cosmetically restored by BR at Stewarts Lane depot prior to their delivery by road from Haywards Heath. Like the arrival of the BR Standard Class 4MT locomotive, the use of Bulleid stock represented another major turning point in the line's history and further erosion of the Bluebell's 'sleepy branch line' image. It should be noted that a rake of BR and Bulleid-designed coaches was used on the Bluebell for a brief period in 1963 when the 'Chesham' set was on loan to London Transport. *Author*

A complete preserved pre-grouping train. In the early years of the Bluebell there was a preponderance among the membership of devotees of the LBSCR who may have found it difficult to accept that the SECR P Class 0-6-0T locomotives, which were only acquired because no 'Terriers' were available, proved a huge success on the short Bluebell trains then being operated. These workhorses were robust, reliable and economical and their capabilities exceeded all expectations. In this picture No.27 is depicted on the ascent of Freshfield bank with a two-coach train, formed of SECR coaches, on 9th August 1970. *Chris Gammell / Bluebell Archive*

1971 In the early 1970s the motive power situation on the Bluebell was dire, this being a legacy of lack of investment in facilities in the 1960s because all available funds were being earmarked for the line purchase scheme. The GWR 'Dukedog' locomotive's tender was in poor condition and had to be withdrawn from service whilst the locomotive itself was fit for traffic. In the case of the SECR C Class 0-6-0 engine, which arrived at the Bluebell in August 1970, the reverse was true, the locomotive was 'stopped' with axle problems but its tender was fit to run. The Railway's locomotive department was desperate for another working engine so it was decided to pair the 'Dukedog' with the C Class tender. The combination may have looked rather peculiar but this simple expedient provided another serviceable locomotive. Here, the 'C-dog', as No.3217 was nicknamed, is seen passing Holywell (Waterworks) with a northbound train on 12th September 1971. *David Clark*

The highlight of the year 1971 was undoubtedly the return to service in early August of BR Standard Class 4MT 4-6-0 No.75027 in fine condition following overhaul. This was a major achievement bearing in mind the locomotive department's chronic lack of facilities. In this illustration No.75027 emits a magnificent smokescreen as it ascends Freshfield bank on a sunny 19th September 1971 with a heavy train in tow. Another momentous event later in the year was the delivery of the largest influx of rolling stock ever seen on the Railway, largely as a result of the collapse of a preservation project at Liss, in Hampshire. This collection included the Bulleid Society's unrestored Pacific No.34023 *Blackmore Vale* (which subsequently entered service as Southern Railway No.21C123) and the Southern Locomotive Preservation Company's USA Class 0-6-0T locomotive No.30064, plus four coaches and various wagons. The latter locomotive was in working order and entered traffic on 20th November. The arrival of these items, and the volunteers who came with them, was a major landmark in the history of the Bluebell. *David Clark*

1972 The centenary of Bluebell's oldest locomotive, 'Terrier' No.72 *Fenchurch*, occurred on 7th September 1972 and plans were laid to commemorate this important milestone in the engine's history. A special booklet was produced and (what was described as) a 'limited edition' of 5,000 mugs in Portmeirion pottery with an outline drawing of the veteran locomotive was commissioned. It was also advertised that a special handstamp would be used on letters posted at Sheffield Park on the 'big' day. Unfortunately, all of the Railway's plans went awry because a general overhaul of No.72 could not be completed in time and, much to the Bluebell's embarrassment, its re-entry into traffic had to be delayed until 5th November. The problem was, apparently, that *Fenchurch* needed a new smokebox door which could not be manufactured in time. Oh dear! In this picture a partially completed No.72 sits under the locomotive shed extension at Sheffield Park on 2nd September 1972. One wonders how long the 5,000 mugs took to sell out! *Chris Gammell / Bluebell Archive*

Sunshine after rain, just perfect for railway photography. The deluge has stopped, the last of the dark clouds has passed over and, magically, everything glistens as the sun suddenly bursts out of the sky. Here the photographer has taken maximum advantage of the brilliant conditions as SECR P Class 0-6-0T No.27, emitting a superb smoke effect, passes Holywell (Waterworks) with a northbound train on 3rd December 1972. A tangible link with the early days of the railway was lost when Bluebell Halt, the original northern terminus of the line, was demolished on 20th February 1972. *Roger Cruse*

1973 In the early 1970s, as previously stated, the Bluebell was suffering from a shortage of serviceable motive power and the decision was taken to send the Adams 'Radial' locomotive No.488 away for repair at Swindon works, the locomotive leaving on 4th October 1971. Initially it was thought that the overhaul would cost around £11,000, but the engine's boiler was found to be in a worse condition than anticipated and this was sent to Crewe because Swindon works was not equipped to undertake the specialist work required. The eventual repair cost was almost £18,000 and some members thought this amount would have been better spent on developing the Bluebell's own locomotive overhaul facility. Everyone agreed, however, that when the locomotive made its first reappearance in traffic it looked absolutely splendid. Its return to service, on 4th August 1973, was marked by a special train for invited guests only and this is pictured at Town House bridge. This low key event, which was criticised by some members, was in total contrast to the amazing scenes that accompanied *Blackmore Vale*'s return to traffic three years later. *David Clark*

1975 The C Class locomotive eventually made its first public appearance working a morning goods train from Sheffield Park to Horsted Keynes on 'Bluebell on Parade' day in 1975. In this illustration No.592, which had yet to be fully restored in the elaborate SECR livery, is depicted approaching Town House bridge with an up train on 8th June 1975, just a few weeks after its welcome return. *David Clark*

Even the sheep grazing in the fields adjoining the Bluebell track must have turned their heads when this weird and wonderful sight appeared charging up the line towards Horsted Keynes on 2nd November 1975: what an amazing spectacle! The locomotive is, of course, Bulleid Pacific No.21C123 *Blackmore Vale* which had arrived on the Bluebell in 1971. Members of the Bulleid Society had toiled ceaselessly, in very primitive conditions, to restore their beloved engine and an inspection by their boiler inspector was arranged for 2nd November. He pronounced himself very satisfied with the steam test so an unscheduled run up the line was hastily arranged for members despite the engine's decidedly unfinished appearance. Here, No.21C123 is seen galloping past Holywell in the sunshine with the former Longmoor Military Railway brake van in tow. One can only imagine the feeling of exhilaration and achievement felt by those who had worked so hard to return *Blackmore Vale* to operation. *Ian Wright*

1976 The changing scene at Sheffield Park. The brand new locomotive works building in the background dominates this view of the USA Class tank engine pausing between duties at Sheffield Park on 28th March 1976. Construction of this large building, which was quickly dubbed 'The Cathedral' by Bluebell staff, was a further huge step forward for the Railway. Finance was largely provided by the 'Loco Shed Appeal Fund' and money was raised from various sources including visitors, who were encouraged to 'buy a brick', and events such as disco dances organised by members. Since this picture was taken the Bluebell's locomotive works has developed into one of the best equipped on any preserved railway in Great Britain. There are two repair roads, both of which have inspection pits along their entire length, and a wheel drop. The adjacent workshop is equipped with a wide range of machinery, including lathes and boring machines. A wheel lathe was installed some while ago but this is not currently operational and wheelsets requiring turning (to reprofile the tyres) are, at the time of writing, despatched to the South Devon Railway at Buckfastleigh. The works used to have a manually operated overhead crane, but this has since been replaced by an electrically operated crane which is much easier to use. The USA Class tank engine is standing next to the former cattle dock which, as its name suggests, was used for loading livestock into covered wagons. These installations were a familiar sight at many country stations when farmers were still dependent on the railways for the movement of animals. *Chris Gammell / Bluebell Archive*

In complete contrast to the Adams locomotive's quiet re-entry into service a few years earlier, *Blackmore Vale*'s return to steam on 15th May 1976 was arguably one of the best-publicised events ever staged on the Bluebell Railway and gained massive coverage in the local and national media. The locomotive was scheduled to work four trains, the first being for invited guests, while two further workings ran during the afternoon to enable the general public to take a ride. In the evening a special train was provided for those who had booked for a disco-dance at Horsted Keynes. It was decided to commemorate the fiftieth anniversary of the 'Atlantic Coast Express' and *Blackmore Vale* plus the coaches were suitably decorated. Appropriately, the train, formed of seven coaches, boasted five of Bulleid design including composite vehicle No.S5768 which is owned by the Bulleid Society. The principal guest was the world-famous artist David Shepherd who unveiled the locomotive's nameplate and new shield prior to the departure of the first train. It was estimated that around 700 members of the public were conveyed during the day plus 300 on board the disco special and everybody agreed it was one of the most successful days ever on the Railway. In this portrait an immaculate *Blackmore Vale* gleams in the evening sun as it heads past Holywell with the twelve-coach disco train in tow. What an unforgettable sight! *Author*

After the triumphant launch of *Blackmore Vale* into traffic on May 15th the locomotive developed a fault and was diagnosed with blowing superheater elements. During the following day, when it was rostered in service once again, it was decided that, as a precaution against a failure out on the line, it would be wise to pilot No.21C123 throughout the day. This defect was a cruel blow to those who had worked on the engine's restoration but at least the many passengers and lineside observers were not disappointed. Here, *Blackmore Vale*, piloted by C Class No.592, ascends Freshfield bank with a train to Horsted Keynes, with the pilot doing most of the work whilst No.21C123 makes a token effort. Perhaps in the past when a Bulleid Pacific has expired on a Dover to Victoria boat train a C Class locomotive has been commandeered to give it a helping hand – who knows? *David Clark*

In addition to No.21C123 *Blackmore Vale* making its first public appearance in service, at least three other locomotives were in traffic to entertain the customers during the weekend of 15th/16th May. In this illustration the Adams 'Radial' No.488 and H Class 0-4-4T No.263 have just left Sheffield Park station and are about to start the climb of Freshfield bank with an afternoon train on 16th May 1976. One wonders if the photographer had arranged the spectacular smoke effects! Unlike the Adams locomotive, the H Class, which was owned by the H Class Trust, was very much a newcomer to the line, having arrived from Ashford on 25th January 1976. It made a trial run on 28th February and was given a clean bill of health with the result that it worked two trains the following day. It subsequently became a very useful locomotive, just the kind of moderately powered engine the railway needed. It was running in unlined condition at that time. Comment was made in 'Bluebell News', the Bluebell Railway's journal, about the increasing SECR presence on the line! *John S. Everitt / Bluebell Archive*

1977 A welcome addition to the Bluebell motive power fleet was Maunsell U Class 2-6-0 No.1618 which arrived from the Kent & East Sussex Railway at Tenterden on 17th May 1977. Constructed in 1928 at Brighton Works, No.1618 had an unremarkable working life at a variety of sheds and was withdrawn in January 1964. It was sold as scrap to Woodham Brothers of Barry, South Wales, and arrived in their yard under its own steam from Fratton on 18th June 1964. It remained there until rescued by the Southern Mogul Preservation Society in 1969 and was initially stored at Aylesford in Kent, before moving to the KESR where restoration took place. It was moved to the Bluebell using the same low loader used to move the Bulleid Q1 Class locomotive from Brighton a few days previously. It was steamed for the first time on Bluebell metals on 24th June 1977 and commenced work on Bluebell passenger trains in the first week of July. The 'Mogul' proved a huge asset to the Railway being free-steaming, versatile and, most importantly, economical and was almost universally liked by footplate crews. In this picture it is seen shortly after leaving Sheffield Park on 28th August 1977. *David Clark*

A scene at Horsted Keynes on 29th August 1977 as P Class No.323 *Bluebell* carries out a shunting manoeuvre with a 'lowmac' wagon and brake van from the erstwhile Longmoor Military Railway. This class was designed for branch line work on motor trains and spent most of its life on these duties until relegated to light shunting and shed pilot work. In the early years of the Bluebell Railway the P Class engines did sterling work whilst at the same time proving reliable and economical in service. At the time of writing two P Class locomotives are undergoing overhaul at Sheffield Park and should have returned to service by the time this album is published. *David Clark*

1978 Compilation of a pictorial record of this type is dependent upon the help and co-operation of many people without whose assistance this album would never have seen the light of day. A reasonable selection of images was submitted for virtually every year covered by the book, but for reasons not immediately apparent to the author there was a dearth of pictures taken in 1978. What was it about this year that apparently deterred Bluebell photographers? Here, on the 18th June of that year, the USA tank locomotive and *Bluebell* emerge from the trees at the approach to Holywell. There is nothing of special significance about this shot ... but at least it was taken in 1978! A major event later that year was the arrival of some locomotives from Barry scrap yard in South Wales, including a BR Standard Class 9F 2-10-0, one of the largest and most powerful engines ever built for service in Great Britain, which emphasised the changing face of the Bluebell Railway. *John Scrace*

1979 Springtime on the Bluebell. The C Class 0-6-0 No.592, assisted by H Class 0-4-4T No.263, takes the 2.45pm Sheffield Park to Horsted Keynes train up Freshfield bank on 15th April 1979. By this date the extremely elaborate lining and lettering of the H Class appears to be almost complete, apart from the SECR crest, whilst similar work on No.592 is clearly proceeding but not quite as advanced. *John Scrace*

The USA tank locomotive gives *Bluebell* a helping hand on Freshfield bank: the pair were working the 1.40pm Sheffield Park to Horsted Keynes train on 13th May 1979. This is a particularly interesting picture because it shows three suburban coaches, in BR 'rail blue' livery, that had been displaced by electrification from the King's Cross suburban services. Latterly, these vehicles were only used during the rush hours and had been maintained on a strictly minimal maintenance basis for some years and were, therefore, in need of a major overhaul when they were purchased. The Bluebell's existing carriage fleet had suffered dreadfully from constant exposure to wind and rain and the coaches were bought in the mid-1970s to give the Carriage & Wagon Dept. some breathing space. They are (from left to right) a composite lavatory vehicle (classified CL), a second lavatory open (SLO) and a brake second (BS). When they arrived all of the coaches were in quite reasonable condition superficially, but after a few years problems arose with corroded door pillars and other parts that were being attacked by large areas of rust, so these carriages proved to be something of a mixed blessing. In the circumstances it was decided that the expensive and time-consuming remedial work necessary to restore them could not be justified and the decision was taken to dispose of the coaches. They were eventually sold and left the Bluebell in 1986. *David Cox*

1980 BR Standard Class 4MT 4-6-0 No.75027 draws the 2.28pm Sheffield Park to Horsted Keynes train up Freshfield bank on 7th April 1980. The locomotive was in resplendent condition after emerging just before Christmas 1979 from overhaul in the Bluebell's locomotive works. The comprehensive repair given to No.75027 took 2½ years to complete and was said to be the most thorough yet undertaken in the Bluebell's workshop including a partial rebuild of the tender. It should, perhaps, be pointed out that Bluebell staff were not working continuously on No.75027 during that time and had a host of other routine jobs to undertake on the engines in service. *John Scrace*

The year 1980 will be best remembered in some quarters for a lightning strike that demolished the chimney of Horsted Keynes signal box on 29th July, whilst others will doubtless recall the delivery of Maunsell 'Schools' Class locomotive No.928 *Stowe,* which arrived from Somerset in mid-July, and its subsequent restoration at lightning speed. The vast majority of Bluebell supporters will, however, probably regard the twentieth anniversary celebrations, which took place during the weekend of 2nd/3rd August, as the highlight of the year. The main attraction was the re-enactment (as far as practicable) of the first train and this was formed of *Fenchurch,* coach Nos. 971 and 6686, plus *Bluebell* on the rear. Two of the Bluebell's founder members were present for the occasion, while other invited people included numerous civic guests and dignitaries plus other 'famous faces' from the preservation world. Some members were in Victorian costume but perhaps regretted their decision to don period dress in view of the blisteringly hot weather. In this picture Mr Johnson, vice chairman of Lewes District Council, endeavours to re-christen *Fenchurch* in the traditional manner, but the bottle failed to break at the first attempt, just like the bottle used twenty years previously at the ceremony to reopen the line in 1960! After 'The Pioneer' had left Sheffield Park at 2.28pm, the next up train was 'The Pines Express' with Donald Beale and Peter Smith, two renowned Somerset and Dorset line enginemen, aboard. This train comprised eight coaches hauled by Maunsell 2-6-0 No.1618 piloted by BR Standard 4-6-0 No.75027, the latter engine being, of course, a former S&D locomotive. *David Cox*

People on the opposite platform admire the immaculately turned-out train at Horsted Keynes station on 2nd August 1980. Note *Bluebell*'s beautifully burnished buffers. The programme on the following day was slightly marred by the failure of *Fenchurch,* for which the Adams 'Radial' tank locomotive No.488 deputised. *R.C. Riley*

1981 The restoration of Maunsell 'Schools' Class 4-4-0 No.928 *Stowe* was probably the most rapid ever carried out on the Bluebell, mainly due to the enthusiasm of the (then) locomotive works manager who had worked on *Stowe* at Bricklayers Arms shed during his BR career. Quite extensive work was undertaken on the engine including removal of all the superheater elements and small tubes from the boiler, renewal of the front of the smokebox and repairs to the ashpan, in addition to a multitude of other essential jobs. No.928 was steamed for the first time after eighteen years of inactivity on 5th June 1981, a magnificent effort considering it only arrived on Bluebell metals on 10th July 1980! *Stowe* was purchased for preservation by Lord Montagu of Beaulieu for display purposes way back in 1963 and was later transferred to the East Somerset Railway. Lord Montagu was the Bluebell Railway's principal guest when it returned to traffic on 13th June 1981 following a naming ceremony at Horsted Keynes station. Later that day it powered the 7.30pm members' special from Sheffield Park which was photographed in glorious evening sunshine at Town House bridge. During the following week No.928 was in continuous service and performed faultlessly apart from a slightly hot middle big end which was soon rectified. *Roger Cruse*

1982 Sussex or Siberia? There was certainly a very cold start to 1982, the year when the Bluebell celebrated the centenary of the Lewes to East Grinstead line. The Bulleid Q1 Class locomotive No.33001 is seen here setting off from Sheffield Park across the snowy wastes of East Sussex with a northbound train on 10th January. No.33001 arrived at the Bluebell, as previously stated, in 1977 on loan from the National Railway Museum. It was one of a class of forty highly unconventional engines built to meet an urgent wartime need for a powerful freight locomotive with wide route availability. The Q1s were devoid of many of the usual features such as running plates, splashers and orthodox boiler cladding, which not only made them cheap to construct but also saved precious materials. In the author's view it is a great shame that many enthusiasts regarded these locomotives as the 'ugly ducklings' of Southern steam when, in reality, they performed the tough job for which they were designed really brilliantly and it could be argued that they were Bulleid's most successful design. *Roger Cruse*

The centenary of the Lewes to East Grinstead line, opened on 1st August 1882, was marked on the Bluebell by a series of major events, visiting locomotives, brake van specials and the running of the 'Centenary Cutler' dining train. On the commercial side a range of centenary souvenirs was produced and, in order to give centenary year a special identity, there was even an immediately recognisable logo that was used on Bluebell advertising and publicity material throughout the year. The year began quietly and the first really tangible event indicating that 1982 was going to be a very special year took place on 24th March when LBSCR 0-4-2 *Gladstone*, of 1882 vintage, arrived on loan from the National Railway Museum, followed by *Sharpthorn* on 3rd April. The latter engine was a truly remarkable survivor that had been used on the construction of the Bluebell line. Another notable event was the completion of restoration work on *Baxter*, an industrial locomotive that came to the Bluebell in 1960. The volunteers involved in its extensive repair had been in a race against time to have it ready for centenary year and here a resplendent *Baxter*, garlanded with flowers, poses at Sheffield Park on 9th May 1982, the second day of 'Bluebell on Parade' weekend. By this time the Bluebell's long-awaited locomotive shed was beginning to take shape in the background. *John Scrace*

The centrepiece of the centenary year calendar was undoubtedly Cavalcade Weekend on 26th/27th June. Billed as '100 Years of History in a Single Day', this was arguably the most ambitious 'show' ever staged by the Bluebell Railway and involved every available locomotive parading through Horsted Keynes station in historical order. Almost unbelievably, thirteen engines were in steam during the weekend, including two 'guest' locomotives, Kent & East Sussex Railway No.25 *Northiam* and Caledonian Railway 0-4-4T No.419 which had come down from Scotland to take part in the celebrations. Visitors who turned up at Sheffield Park station while the cavalcades were taking place would have been shocked to find the locomotive shed almost deserted! The cavalcade weekend attracted vast crowds of spectators to Horsted Keynes, but by the time this picture was taken on the evening of 27th June most had, apparently, left for home and the photographer was able to record this unrepeatable line-up of locomotives. *John Beckett*

The cavalcades were the culmination of months of meticulous planning by Bluebell management and volunteers who earned the gratitude and admiration of many of the onlookers visiting Horsted Keynes during the weekend. The cavalcades involved an unprecedented number of light engine movements between Sheffield Park and Horsted Keynes which had to be slotted in between the scheduled passenger trains. One wonders how many Bluebell locomotive crews were required to be on duty during the weekend. This picture was taken from Leamland bridge, just north of Horsted Keynes station, on 27th June. The breakdown crane, on the right, which was purchased from Newton Heath shed, Manchester, arrived at the Railway in November 1981. It subsequently proved to be something of a white elephant and has been stored unserviceable for many years. *John Beckett*

It was extremely unfortunate that after all the careful planning that went into organising the centenary weekend, the Bluebell was hit by appalling bad luck on the afternoon of 27th June when a broken rail was found near Freshfield. Such occurrences are very rare and for this to happen during a major event was a real blow. A party of permanent way staff was immediately despatched from Horsted Keynes but, even so, no trains ran for over two hours while emergency work was carried out, and the extent of the disruption can be gauged from the fact that after the arrival of a train at Horsted Keynes at 3.20pm, the next train from Sheffield Park arrived at 6.04pm. The two cavalcades had taken place roughly as advertised, but it was clear that many passengers making their way to Horsted Keynes had been stranded at Sheffield Park and a third cavalcade was hastily arranged for them, so nobody was disappointed. Some of the locomotives were running dry and had their tanks topped up with water pumped from the fire train's tank wagons. The manner in which Bluebell staff responded to the situation was widely praised and earned the gratitude of many spectators. Needless to say, the locomotive workings were totally disrupted and at around 6.00pm on the Sunday evening Horsted Keynes contained fifteen engines, of which thirteen were in steam. The Railway's management resorted to unprecedented measures in order to get the locomotives back to Sheffield Park and it was decided that the 6.35pm from Horsted Keynes would be quintuple headed. The train is seen at Freshfield, the weary locomotive crews no doubt relieved that their unexpectedly long day was almost over. *John Beckett*

The sun bursts through a chink in the otherwise overcast sky as Caledonian Railway 0-4-4T No.419 assists SECR C Class No.592 on the climb of Freshfield bank in July 1982. The lovely Caledonian engine, which is the property of the Scottish Railway Preservation Society, arrived at the Bluebell on 19th May for the entire summer period. *Matthew Cousins*

LBSCR 0-4-2 No.214 *Gladstone* sits in the Pump House siding at Sheffield Park on 18th July 1982. This shot was taken during a specially arranged photographic session and the enthusiasts involved wanted their pictures to have as much 'Victorian authenticity' as possible, so an intrusive floodlight on the corner of the pump house building was temporarily removed. No.214, as previously mentioned, was built at Brighton Works in 1882 to the design of William Stroudley and amassed well over a million miles during its career which ended in 1927. It would probably have been cut-up, but was preserved as a result of the intervention of the Stephenson Locomotive Society and later passed into the custody of the British Transport Commission. It is now in the care of the National Railway Museum at York. Unfortunately, *Gladstone* was not in operational condition but, even so, was a very popular static exhibit during the Bluebell's centenary celebrations. *Roger Cruse*

Inevitably, perhaps, some of the locomotives that the Bluebell originally intended to bring to the railway during centenary year failed to materialise. The LSWR Beattie well tank, then based at Quainton Road in Buckinghamshire, could not be repaired in time while the planned visit of *Flying Scotsman* had to be shelved due to the high cost of transport from its Carnforth base. The Railway had requested the use of the National Railway Museum's replica *Rocket,* plus the open Liverpool & Manchester Railway carriage with which it operates, but it was delayed by a dock strike in Australia and for a time it seemed that the Bluebell might be disappointed. It had been the intention that *Rocket* would head the processions but during the cavalcade weekend it was still on the high seas *en route* to Great Britain. *Rocket,* described by one member as 'the most modern steam engine on the railway', eventually arrived on 30th July, just in time for the Line Centenary Weekend and fortunately the late John Bellwood, from the National Railway Museum, was on hand to instruct Bluebell engine crews in the intricacies of driving the contraption. Some lucky visitors had the privilege of riding behind *Rocket* over the full length of the line, but most had to be content with a short ride along the up headshunt at Horsted Keynes, as seen here. Other significant events during 1982 included *Stepney*'s return to steam on 11th September while the usual Vintage Transport event took place on the following day. The Bulleid Society celebrated the centenary of O.V.S. Bulleid on the weekend of September 18th/19th. What a year! *Ian Wright*

1983 In the early 1980s, prior to the expiration of its boiler certificate, the Adams 'Radial' tank locomotive No.488 ran for a brief period in BR black livery as No.30583. The repaint was largely undertaken by photographers who had also bought the paint(!), so the transformation was carried out at no cost to the Bluebell. The aim was, of course, to attempt to recreate scenes of the Axminster to Lyme Regis branch where members of this class worked for many years. On summer Saturdays Lyme Regis trains conveyed through main-line coaches from Waterloo so this shot is reasonably representative of the branch. Here, No.30583 makes a splendid sight, and throws a considerable smokescreen across the Sussex countryside, as it approaches Three Arch bridge, just south of Horsted Keynes, with the 2.45pm train *ex*-Sheffield Park on 5th March 1983. Two months later No.30583 developed firebox problems and had to be withdrawn from service, its final day in traffic apparently being 11th May. *Graham Mallinson*

David and Goliath. Much to the amazement of onlookers the diminutive *Baxter* expends its maximum possible effort and manages to get *Blackmore Vale* on the move during shunting operations at Sheffield Park on 7th May 1983. A month after this picture was taken *Baxter* met with an unfortunate accident when it was on its way home from a model railway show in Croydon, where it had been on display. It broke loose from its fastenings and toppled off its low loader onto the road, sustaining considerable damage. Fortunately, the damage was soon rectified, and *Baxter* was quickly back on its feet, so to speak. It is one of the oldest engines in the Bluebell fleet, having emerged from Fletcher Jennings works at Whitehaven, Cumberland, way back in 1877 and is the sole surviving standard gauge engine built by that firm. It worked at the Dorking Greystone Lime Company's works at Betchworth until 1960 when it was placed on loan to the Bluebell and it has since been purchased by the Bluebell Railway so this attractive little locomotive can remain permanently at Sheffield Park. *David Cox*

Few locomotives at the Bluebell have had such a low profile as the SECR P Class 0-6-0T No.31178. It was sold out of service by BR to Bowaters, Sittingbourne, in 1957, subsequently declared 'surplus to requirements' in 1969, and acquired by the Bluebell. Unfortunately, the locomotive was in need of a general repair and, even worse, its arrival at Sheffield Park coincided with a reduced requirement for small tank locomotives and consequently it languished out of use for many years. In the early 1980s it was cosmetically restored as BR No.31178 and is seen here at Sheffield Park on 8th May 1983 looking rather smart, to say the least. Alas, its 'beauty' was just skin deep! No.31178 has since experienced a dramatic change of fortune, however, and at the time of writing is nearing the end of a long and protracted overhaul which will see it come out of the cold and be part of the Bluebell's working fleet for the first time. *David Cox*

1984 The splendid Sussex countryside at its best! *Stepney* takes a southbound train through the lovely Wealden landscape at Tremaines on 28th January 1984, a beautifully clear winter's day. This shot exemplifies the ever-changing Bluebell scene, because Otye bridge has been filled-in since this picture was taken and, furthermore, encroachment of trees and undergrowth has made it almost impossible to photograph trains from this position today. A number of bridges on the Bluebell Railway have been demolished or infilled over the years to save expenditure on repairs, a move regretted by a number of members who consider the line has been robbed of some of its character and history.
Chris Gammell / Bluebell Archive

Black beauty. One of the Bluebell's objectives from the earliest days of the line was acquisition of a BR Standard Class 4MT 2-6-4T locomotive, a class that had been designed and built at Brighton works and was especially associated with the line's closing years. The Bluebell earmarked No.80154, the last locomotive constructed at Brighton and the engine that hauled the final BR passenger working along the Bluebell in 1958. Very sadly, when this locomotive became available in April 1967, the Bluebell was desperately trying to raise funds to buy the line and the Railway's management was in no position to even consider purchasing No.80154, which was scrapped six months later. In 1983, however, the '80064 Locomotive Group', then based on the Dart Valley Railway, wanted a new home and approached the Bluebell with the result that the stirring sight and sound of one of these engines was heard once again on the line. Built in 1953, No.80064 had been based at Watford Junction, Tonbridge and Bristol (Barrow Road) during its BR career, which ended in September 1965. During its nine years-long restoration in Devon a complete air braking system was fitted to the locomotive and part of its air pump is just visible on the left of the smokebox. It entered Bluebell service on 16th June 1984 and is pictured on the 2.50pm Sheffield Park to Horsted Keynes train at Ketches Farm on 29th July 1984. *John Scrace*

In mid-1984 the Bulleid Society decided to repaint No.21C123 *Blackmore Vale* in BR 1950s livery for the last months of its boiler ticket and it made its debut in BR colours on 28th July 1984 working the 'Bluebell Cutler'. Needless to say, this decision was acclaimed by numerous photographers who were brought up in the BR era! Unfortunately, at that time Great Britain was in the grip of a miners' strike and the Bluebell was anxious to preserve coal stocks, so No.34023 did not operate as frequently as had been hoped but it was able to work during a steam gala in September. *Blackmore Vale's* last run in BR livery was reportedly on a normal service train on 14th October. A major development in 1984 was the Bluebell's purchase of the station site at Kingscote which unexpectedly came onto the market, so the Railway found itself in the strange position of owning both the West Hoathly (bought in 1975) and Kingscote sites but none of the land in between. In addition, the year 1984 saw the skill and dedication of members of the Carriage & Wagon Department officially recognised when Maunsell Open Third coach No.1309 won the Association of Railway Preservation Societies' prestigious 'Coach of the Year' award. The vehicle was purchased in 1973 and served as a mess coach for several years before restoration commenced in earnest in 1981. *Ian Wright*

1985 The changing face of Sheffield Park station. In times gone by there was a footbridge at the north end of Sheffield Park station, but it was demolished in about 1953, and ever since passengers wishing to cross the running lines were obliged to use a foot crossing. The ever-increasing popularity of the Bluebell Railway meant that the crossing became very busy at peak times, in stark contrast to the trickle of passengers during the dying years of the BR regime, and this highlighted the safety issues involved. The obvious answer was a new footbridge and the Bluebell lost no time in buying the former racegoers' footbridge (which is twelve feet wide) from Lingfield when it became available. The bridge was craned into position on 22nd March 1985 and in this picture, taken on 31st March, work is proceeding on concreting the base of the structure in place. There was a massive amount of work to be done before the footbridge could be brought into use and the official opening eventually took place on 28th June 1986. Appropriately, the opening ceremony was performed by the late Ernie Moore who had supervised people using the foot crossing at Sheffield Park for many years. *David Cox*

The 11.00am train to Sheffield Park sets off from Horsted Keynes station on 13th July 1985. At that time the Bluebell was able to assemble a rake of five Bulleid coaches which form most of the train – the remaining vehicle is a BR Standard Mk1 coach. The leading engine is the North London Railway 0-6-0T locomotive No.58850, which previously ran on the Bluebell as No.2650, making a welcome return to traffic in its new guise in 1984 after a very long period of inactivity. The immediately recognisable train engine is *Bluebell*. The year 1985 was a momentous one in the history of the line and Bluebell members were jubilant when the government announced its approval of the Railway's extension plans. *John Scrace*

1986

The B4 Class 0-4-0 Dock Tank locomotive No.96 *Normandy* was built by the LSWR at Nine Elms in November 1893 for shunting purposes. A total of twenty-five engines of this class was built and in their twilight years they could be found at such far-flung locations as Dover, Bournemouth, Plymouth and Eastleigh, so they were very widely dispersed. One or two were sold for industrial use and worked even further afield from their usual haunts. The class was particularly associated with Southampton docks where a total of fourteen examples was based until replaced by USA Class 0-6-0Ts in 1947. No.96 was one of a batch of ten constructed especially for work in the docks at Southampton and originally ran with an open-sided cab until this was enclosed as an air raid precaution. It ended its career with BR as No.30096 in October 1963, its last duty being to shunt the tightly-curved goods yard at Winchester. Following withdrawal, No.30096 was purchased by Messrs. Corralls, the fuel merchants, for further use at Dibles Wharf, Southampton, where it was christened *Corrall Queen*. It survived there for some years until purchased by the B4 Locomotive Group in December 1972: it is now the property of the Bulleid Society. After a protracted repair which saw the engine's open cab restored, No.96 returned to active use on 2nd August 1986 and is seen here at Three Arch bridge hauling a special 9.30am Sheffield Park to Horsted Keynes goods train which was run for the benefit of photographers. *John Scrace*

Apart from the entry of *Normandy* into service, the year 1986 may not have been the most noteworthy for developments regarding locomotives and rolling stock, but in many other respects was a momentous one. On 15th March the Bluebell launched a share issue in connection with the extension to East Grinstead at a ceremony at Sheffield Park station. Special guests included the Chairman and Vice-Chairman of Mid Sussex District Council and the Town Mayor of East Grinstead. This was accompanied by a fanfare of publicity in the media and was a resounding success, the

minimum subscription being reached with fifteen days to spare. The share issue eventually closed at the end of March 1987 by which time the magnificent total of £461,630 had been raised – a splendid achievement. Another major event during 1986 was the opening of the new buffet building costing £224,000, for which the Bluebell were awarded a 15% grant by the English Tourist Board. The Railway's catering staff had laboured for years in totally inadequate, cramped converted carriages but all that changed on 9th July when the new buffet opened for business. The kitchen was extended in 1997 and the building was further extended in 2004 to house the new shop with administrative offices above. All of these developments were designed to harmonise as much as possible with the style of the existing buildings. The new catering block is seen here on 29th June 1986, two days after being officially handed over by the builders. *David Cox*

1987 'The Bluebell Railway regret that due to severe weather conditions services maybe subject to delay or cancellation'. In reality, when nature conspired to make things difficult, the Bluebell operating staff were all the more determined to run the advertised service, even if the number of passengers could be counted on the fingers of one hand! Despite the sub-zero temperatures, staff certainly rose to the challenge on 11th January 1987, and in this picture the North London tank locomotive, assisted by the B4 Class 0-4-0T No.96, blasts its way up Freshfield bank as the sun shines brightly out of a clear blue sky. There was a locomotive at each end of the train to avoid problems with frozen points at Horsted Keynes. Could that be a passenger sitting in the front coach – surely not? *Ian Wright*

1988 In March 1988 the Bluebell commemorated the closure of the original Lewes to East Grinstead route by disguising BR Standard Class 4MT 2-6-4T No.80064 as 'No.80154', the last steam engine built at Brighton works and the locomotive that hauled the final BR train along the line on 16th March 1958. In order to make No.80064 look the part its air pump was removed from the right hand side of the smokebox and a new numberplate was specially manufactured. 'No.80154' was in service on 13th March 1988, the day on which the (then) Secretary of State for Transport, the Rt. Hon. Paul Channon MP, ceremonially laid the first track panel for the Northern Extension just north of Leamland bridge, Horsted Keynes. This historic event gave the project a great start and the laying of the first panel was tangible proof that the scheme to extend to East Grinstead really was on its way. A few weeks later 'No.80154' paraded up and down the line with a single coach for photographers, thus recreating the last days of operation under the BR regime. It is seen here in Lindfield Wood on a gloriously sunny 31st March 1988. *Mike Esau*

Those members who were taken aback by the arrival of BR Standard Class 4MT No.75027 in 1969, which at the time was the largest engine ever seen on Bluebell Railway metals, must have stared in total disbelief when Bulleid 'Merchant Navy' Class 8P No.35027 *Port Line* arrived at Sheffield Park on loan on 31st May 1988. No.35027 entered traffic in late 1948 and spent the first five years of its life at Stewarts Lane shed before moving to the Western Section where it worked until withdrawn in September 1966. It was acquired for preservation by the Port Line Locomotive Project in 1982 and was initially moved to the Swindon and Cricklade Railway. *Port Line* was later transferred to Swindon works where restoration proceeded at an astonishing pace, the engine being steamed for the first time in preservation on 16th April 1988. It had been the group's intention to undertake running-in at the Swanage Railway, but civil engineering problems there thwarted those plans and it was agreed that running-in could take place at the Bluebell Railway. In this picture No.35027 is seen making light work of hauling a six-coach test train at the approach to Horsted Keynes distant signal on 13th June 1988, just five days before its debut in public service. *Ian Wright*

1990

time of this [...]
building whic[...]
planned at th[...]
locomotive w[...]
floor walkwa[...]

The Bluebell commemorated the twenty-fifth anniversary of the closure of the Havant to Hayling Island branch on 5th/6th November 1988 for which an intensive two or three-coach train service was operated using, almost needless to say, the Railway's vintage LBSCR 0-6-0T 'Terriers'. In order to make the event as realistic as possible it was decided it would be sensible to have both locomotives in BR livery (*Fenchurch* had already been repainted as BR No.32636) and some members made the inspired suggestion that *Stepney* should be disguised as the Brighton works shunter No.DS 377 (later No.32635), which ran in Stroudley livery with 'Brighton Works' emblazoned upon its side tanks right up until withdrawal in 1963. The metamorphosis was realised by attaching pre-prepared fablon sheets that were held in place by vaseline. The sheets could, of course, be removed after the event without damaging the paintwork. Both locomotives were due for a boiler examination a few weeks prior to the anniversary and the event was almost cancelled at the last minute because of the indisposition of the Bluebell's boiler inspector. Luckily, another member of the company's staff was able to undertake the work. The event proved hugely popular and boosted the railway's takings on what would otherwise have been a quiet weekend. Here, 'No.DS 377' makes an energetic ascent of the 1 in 75 gradient near Holywell with the 2.10pm Sheffield Park to Horsted Keynes train on 6th November. *David Cox*

198

The train
class acc
subsequ
selected
grind! D

Work on the first stage of the extension, from Horsted Keynes to Horsted House Farm, proceeded throughout 1988 and it was originally hoped that a shuttle service on this section could be introduced during the following year. Unfortunately, the introduction of passenger trains (known as the 'shuttle') on this new section was delayed by the Department of Transport's stipulation that the shuttle operation must be independent from the rest of the Railway and this necessitated considerable track and signalling work at Horsted Keynes which could not be accomplished in time. In addition the lack of a run-round loop at the terminus meant that trains had to be propelled in the northbound direction, and to ensure complete safety Maunsell coach No.S6575 was specially turned and fitted with an observation window plus communication with the driver. The shuttle was eventually inaugurated on 13th April 1990 and in this portrait SECR P Class No.323 *Bluebell* is seen drifting down from Horsted House Farm towards Leamland bridge on the following day which was the first full day of operation. Not surprisingly, the chance to ride over a 'new' section of track proved an irresistible attraction with the general public and an incredible 8,000 journeys were recorded in the twelve days following reopening. *David Cox*

1991 BR Standard Class 9F 2-10-0 No.92240 – a true giant of steam. The Bluebell Railway Class 9F Preservation Group was instigated in 1977 by a small group of members who proved to be adept at relieving people of their hard-earned cash through a combination of (what could be loosely termed) pleading, arm-twisting and friendly hints of the consequences if they did not pay up! Their efforts were also assisted by cash raised from waste paper collection which proved to be a real money-spinner. In little over a year the staggering total of £12,500 was raised, of which £10,500 was earmarked towards the purchase of No.92240, this being achieved on 12th September 1978. A tender chassis costing £800 was also acquired together with some spares obtained from the East Somerset Railway, home of sister engine No.92203 *Black Prince*. The 9F arrived on Bluebell metals on 6th October 1978. Restoration of such a huge locomotive from Barry 'scrap' condition was never going to be easy, especially bearing in mind the fact that a new tender body had to be fabricated, but the 9F team set about the task with incredible enthusiasm. The two large side plates were made up by a firm in Erith at a cost of £1,865, and within a year the 'incredible hulk' was beginning to look like a locomotive once again. Work continued at a less frantic pace throughout the 1980s and No.92240 was steamed for the first time in preservation on 5th September 1990, its official return to traffic taking place on 15th/16th September. All of the arm-twisting had been worthwhile! Here, the 9F approaches Freshfield with the 2.33pm Sheffield Park to Horsted Keynes train in tow on 12th May 1991 during 'Bluebell on Parade' weekend. The rake of Mk1 coaches forming the train was on hire to the Bluebell. *Graham Mallinson*

Photographed on a still, misty morning, Maunsell Q Class 0-6-0 No.541 leaves an impressive smoke trail over the fields as it departs from Sheffield Park with a 'Santa Special' Christmas train in December 1991. Banking assistance is provided by the North London tank locomotive No.58850. Built at Eastleigh in 1939, No.541 led an uneventful life mainly on freight work until withdrawn by BR from Guildford shed in November 1964. The locomotive was despatched to Barry scrap yard until purchased by the 'Southern Q Fund' (which later became part of the Maunsell Society) in 1973 and was initially stabled at Ashchurch in Gloucestershire where restoration commenced. No.541 was moved to the Bluebell, arriving at Sheffield Park in October 1978. It officially returned to steam accompanied by the usual celebrations on 19th November 1983, thus becoming the first of the Railway's collection of 'Barry engines' to be fully restored. In service No.541 proved to be a very powerful locomotive and apparently hauled an eight-coach 'Santa Special' with ease. *Tony Eaton*

1992 The early months of 1992 saw feverish activity on the second stage of the East Grinstead extension, from near Horsted House farm to New Coombe bridge. Work began in earnest on 20th January and for the next nine weeks track-laying proceeded as fast as possible, and by the end of the sixth week track had been laid up to the south end of West Hoathly tunnel. Work continued in the tunnel in appallingly wet and gloomy conditions and on 5th March 1992 the volunteers had very good reason to celebrate when the first train since 1964 passed through and emerged into daylight at the north end. What an achievement! The team was assisted by caterpillar tractors, a Hymac mechanical digger and, latterly, a hired Plasser-Theurer tamper-liner machine, but much of the work still had to be done manually in the traditional way. A run-round had to be provided at West Hoathly and this was completed by 26th March when the final key was hammered into place. Timetabled public services to New Coombe bridge commenced on 17th April, followed by a ceremony marking the official re-opening of West Hoathly tunnel on 16th May. This picture, taken at Courtland Wood on 7th February 1992, gives an indication of the work in progress at that date with the B4 Class 0-4-0T *Normandy* prominent in the foreground on the works train. In the background the Hymac can be seen in action while piles of ballast wait to be laid. *David Cox*

1993 Work in progress on stage three of the Extension, the construction of New Coombe bridge, on 13th March 1993. The bridge was originally used at Llandudno Junction, in North Wales, as (what was officially termed) a 'materials discharge facility' to receive rail-borne loads of aggregate in connection with the A55 road improvement scheme. Materials were discharged into waiting lorries which then took their loads on to the site of the work. Installation of the structure at New Coombe was not without its difficulties, not least when the contractor engaged to undertake piling suddenly went into liquidation! It had been originally intended to install the bridge around Christmas 1992, but various delays meant that the centre span was not lifted into place until 10th May 1993, another 'red letter day' for the extension team. The bridge cost around £43,000 to purchase and install; it was estimated that if the project had been carried out by contractors the total cost would have been in the region of £200,000. The locomotive which is discernible in the background is Maunsell 'Mogul' No.1618. *David Cox*

The year 1993 was also the first full year in service of Maunsell S15 Class 4-6-0 No.847 which is depicted here passing Holywell waterworks with the 10.15am Sheffield Park to Horsted Keynes train on 10th April. Constructed at Eastleigh in December 1936, No.847 was the *very last* 4-6-0 locomotive to be built by the Southern Railway. Withdrawn from traffic by BR in January 1964, No.847 had the good fortune to be sent to Barry scrap yard where it lay until earmarked for preservation by the 847 Locomotive Preservation Fund, which later became part of the Maunsell Society. No.847 arrived at the Bluebell from Barry on 12th October 1978 and restoration started in earnest in 1983. After nine years of toil the locomotive was lit up for the first time in preservation on 10th November 1992 and three days later hauled a special train for Bluebell working members. It entered full public service on 15th November when many favourable comments were received regarding the fine standard of restoration. *Chris Gammell / Bluebell archive*

1994 During early 1994 LSWR M7 Class 0-4-4T No.30053, which is based at the Swanage Railway, was on loan to the Bluebell, a visit that was almost universally welcomed by photographers because it faced southwards and therefore provided a different range of photographic opportunities from a locomotive facing northwards. Perhaps No.30053's most notable claim to fame is the fact that it was shipped to the Steamtown Railway Museum in Vermont, USA in 1967 and remained across the Atlantic until rescued by the Southern Repatriation Group in 1987, so it is a widely travelled engine! Here a nicely groomed No.30053 threads Lindfield Wood with the 1.39pm Horsted Keynes to Sheffield Park train on a bright 12th February 1994, a day when the line north of Horsted Keynes was apparently closed for engineering works in connection with the Northern Extension. *Roger Cruse*

One would have thought that after nearly twenty years of negotiations with landowners, planning inquiries, fund raising and suchlike, not to mention the hard physical work involved in track-laying, mother nature would have been kind to the Bluebell on the official re-opening day of the extension to Kingscote. Alas, no! In this portrait No.592, specially decorated for the occasion, is seen arriving with the official re-opening train in heavy rain on 21st May 1994. The first Bluebell passenger train to reach Kingscote had actually been run a month earlier, on 23rd April, also with No.592 in charge. Track-laying on the section from New Coombe bridge to Kingscote, stage four of the extension project, commenced on 10th January 1994 and was plagued by exceptionally wet weather conditions (just like the re-opening day!) but, even so, reasonable progress was made resulting in LSWR B4 0-4-0T *Normandy,* which powered most of the works trains from Horsted Keynes, being able to pose outside Kingscote booking office on 19th March. The outlay on this phase of the extension was £255,000, slightly under the estimated cost. All of the track and signalling work was passed by the Department of Transport's Inspector on 19th April and the rest, as they say, is history! *Ian Wright*

1995 Truly a peaceful scene as the last rays of the sun illuminate SECR C Class 0-6-0 No.592 passing Holywell on a still February afternoon. *Tony Eaton*

Even on the best-organised preserved railways things sometimes do not go according to plan and on 2nd April 1995 the Bluebell was clearly in the grip of a temporary motive power shortage. This resulted in the 'Golden Arrow' Pullman dining train being hauled by *Bluebell* with B4 Class 0-4-0T *Normandy* as pilot engine, a most extraordinary combination, and probably one unlikely to be repeated. The luxurious Pullman cars are formed at the rear of the train, the first two vehicles being BR Standard Mk1 former Travelling College coaches in chocolate and cream livery. One of these had been extensively modified prior to its arrival on the Bluebell and had a 'lounge' area with a small counter: on the Bluebell it was marketed as the 'New Century Lounge'. The other vehicle was a former dormitory coach which was being utilised as a brake vehicle at the time. Both coaches had been repainted at the Bluebell to match the Pullman train. The train is depicted passing over Otye bridge, heading southwards for Sheffield Park. One wonders if any of the passengers were aware that they were participating in what was actually quite a historic event! *Ian Wright*

Bathed in early morning sunshine, Maunsell 'King Arthur' Class 4-6-0 No.30777 *Sir Lamiel* emerges from West Hoathly tunnel during a photographic charter on 21st August 1995. The visit of *Sir Lamiel,* which was supposed to be the main attraction during the 35th anniversary celebrations on 5th August, was fraught with problems not of the Bluebell's making which resulted in the locomotive being unloaded at precisely the time the guests were arriving for the anniversary events! The engine's whistle was damaged whilst *en route* to the Bluebell and this needed specialist attention from the owners because the locomotive had a main line ticket at that time. There were also other difficulties and this meant that very little use was made of *Sir Lamiel* apart from photographic charters, as seen here. The highlight of the 35th anniversary for those who fancy the occasional tipple was the celebration ale produced especially for the Bluebell by a local brewery. A limited edition of eight hundred half pints was bottled with a full colour label depicting the locomotive *Bluebell. Chris Gammell / Bluebell Archives*

1996 Some of the most attractive Wealden scenery on the Bluebell is found just north of Horsted Keynes and this forms the backdrop to this view of gleaming BR Standard Class 5MT 4-6-0 No.73082 *Camelot,* seen heading north on a bright morning in early 1996. No.73082's pristine appearance is due to the fact that it had been in traffic only a short time following a comprehensive overhaul from Barry scrap yard condition. *Camelot* was one of a class of 172 locomotives turned out over a period of six years; No.73082 was built at Derby and entered service at Stewarts Lane shed, in south London, in June 1955, employed principally on Kent coast trains. In 1959 it was displaced by electrification and moved to nearby Nine Elms shed for use on services from Waterloo to Weymouth. In the same year the Southern Region decided to revive the names of withdrawn 'King Arthur' class engines and No.73082 was allocated the name formerly carried by No.30742. It was withdrawn from traffic on 19th June 1966 and banished to Messrs. Woodham's Barry scrap yard before being purchased by the Camelot Locomotive Society in early 1979, arriving at the Bluebell on 26th October. After many years of endeavour by volunteers the magic moment came at 4.20pm on 16th October 1995 when *Camelot* moved under its own power for the first time in preservation – a great occasion! Its official launch into service took place on 28th October 1995. *Camelot* is very similar to a Stanier 'Black Five', so is unquestionably the author's favourite Bluebell locomotive, so let us hope this splendid machine soon returns to active use. *Author*

Bluebell time! When the lineside bluebells are in full bloom the Bluebell Line really does live up to its name, as seen here in this view taken on 21st May 1996. SECR H Class 0-4-4T No.263 has just passed the erstwhile Ketches Halt and begins the climb of Freshfield bank with a train for Kingscote. The halt was built to serve an attraction set up by a local farmer, but in the event was only open for a short period. The Bluebell Railway has had a number of small stations (known as halts) over the years, namely Freshfield, Holywell (Waterworks) and Bluebell, but all have closed. This has given rise to the rather unkind assertion that the Bluebell has been responsible for more station closures per mile than any other line in the country. The H Class locomotive is now owned by the Bluebell Railway Trust. *Author*

Thunder in Courtland Wood. The mighty BR Standard Class 9F 2-10-0 No.92240 shatters the peace and tranquillity of Courtland Wood as it hastens towards West Hoathly tunnel with a Sheffield Park to Kingscote train on 25th May 1996. Like the locomotive hauling them, the first four carriages are of BR Standard design and they are followed by a Bulleid-designed vehicle. The coach bringing up the rear will be immediately recognised by readers – it is, almost needless to say, the distinctive LNWR observation car. One wonders how many miles the last-mentioned coach has clocked up since coming to the Bluebell in 1963. *Author*

Photographed on an unseasonally cold day in May 1996, the H Class 0-4-4T No.263 is momentarily glimpsed between the trees as it passes over a bridge across a farm track on the climb up Freshfield bank. The locomotive's elaborate SECR livery can be seen in this portrait. At the time of writing No.263 is in the throes of an overhaul in Sheffield Park locomotive works, so let us hope this attractive machine is back in service before too long. *Author*

An industrial branch? The Bluebell Railway is famous for its sleepy, idyllic branch line atmosphere, the only real exceptions to this being the industrial estate adjoining Sheffield Park station, and where the line passes the timber and builders merchant's yard at Kingscote, which provides quite a different backdrop to that found elsewhere on the line. Here, on 21st September 1996, *Baxter* is seen shunting with the timber yard and sawmill in the background, thus creating a scene that could easily be mistaken as one taken on an industrial branch many years ago. At that time the track terminated at the buffer stop seen just beyond the brake van, so this scene is now of considerable historical interest as it has changed considerably since this shot was taken. Note the two nicely restored wagons forming *Baxter's* train, the first one being a banana van while the second wagon is of LBSCR origin as indicated by the initials. *Author*

1997 'Thomas the Tank Engine' weekends were a regular part of the Bluebell calendar for many years, but the Bluebell discontinued 'A day out with Thomas' events following the imposition by the firm owning the rights of new conditions that the Bluebell considered were too onerous. The last 'Thomas' events took place in 2007, being replaced by 'Family Fun Weekends' which were reasonably successful and not so expensive to organise. When this shot of Maunsell S15 Class No.847, piloted by No.1 *Thomas*, was taken near Three Arch bridge in June 1997 these events still attracted huge numbers of participants and virtually every available locomotive and carriage had to be pressed into service to carry the passengers on an intensive timetable – it was a really slick operation. Before it became famous No.1 *Thomas*, which was built in 1939 by the North British Locomotive Co. in Glasgow (NBL No.24564), worked at various collieries in the Midlands before being sold to the Quainton Railway Society in December 1970. *Thomas* is still based at Quainton and frequently travels to other railways for 'Thomas the Tank Engine' events. *Ian Wright*

Mist is hanging in the air as BR Standard Class 4MT 4-6-0 No.75027 takes the 'Golden Arrow' Pullman dining train up the last stretch towards West Hoathly tunnel on a golden autumn day in 1997. The operation of a Pullman train was one of the Bluebell's principal objectives from the earliest days but the dream did not become reality until the early 1990s when the first Pullman coach, *Fingall,* became available after restoration from a semi-derelict state. At the time of writing the operational Pullman fleet comprises three vehicles, Kitchen First *Fingall,* (built in 1924), Third *Christine* (1928) and Third *Lilian,* also built in 1928. It should be noted that the last two cars mentioned were formerly known as Nos. 64 and 76 respectively. The Bluebell's Pullman train has justifiably earned an excellent reputation and frequently runs fully booked – what better recommendation could one wish for? After all, could there be a better or more enjoyable experience than to dine in a sumptuous, beautifully restored Pullman car as it passes through glorious Wealden scenery? In addition to scheduled services the Pullman train is always in demand for wedding day specials and other private charters. *Author*

Photographed on a crisp winter's day with lovely puffy clouds scudding across the sky, BR Standard Class 2MT 2-6-0 No.78022 attacks the climb of Freshfield bank with a train bound for Kingscote. The 'Mogul', which was on loan from the Keighley & Worth Valley Railway, West Yorkshire, proved to be an excellent performer and was capable of hauling five coaches to Kingscote. Whilst the visit of No.78022 was widely welcomed, perhaps the highlight of the year 1997 for many Bluebell members was the acquisition on loan of the SECR O1 Class 0-6-0 No.65, an engine that had not been seen in public for many years. *Author*

Full blast! *Camelot* expends a mighty effort as it heaves a Christmas 'Santa Special' train past Horsted House farm on a freezing morning in December 1997. From modest beginnings, the Bluebell's Christmas train operation has grown considerably over the years and 'Santa Specials' now operate during every pre-Christmas weekend in December, plus a few extra days immediately prior to the bank holiday period. The author clearly remembers the deafening exhaust sound being emitted from *Camelot*'s chimney as it passed his vantage point. *Author*

1998 *Above:* Shenanigans at Horsted Keynes! Temporarily sporting its BR number for the benefit of the photographic fraternity, Bulleid Q1 Class 0-6-0 No.33001 poses for the gathered multitude during a photographic charter on the evening of 13th March 1998. In order to give a little extra colour to the pictures, not to mention entertainment value, some shredded paper was thrown onto the engine's fire and as a result a cascade of sparks showers from the Q1's chimney, producing an effect like a Roman candle firework. One shudders to think what Mr Bulleid would have thought of such frivolity. *David Cox*

Opposite top: During the weekend of 14th/15th March 1998 the Bluebell Railway commemorated the 40th anniversary of the closure of the Lewes to East Grinstead line which occurred on 16th March 1958. BR Standard Class 4MT 2-6-4T No.80080, which was on loan to the Bluebell from the Midland Railway Centre at Butterley, Derbyshire, was suitably disguised as 'No.80154', the last locomotive built at Brighton works and the engine that hauled the final working down the line on that fateful day in 1958. Here it is seen coasting downhill on a Kingscote to Sheffield Park train at Courtland Wood, between West Hoathly tunnel and Vaux End, on 14th March. Note that the first three vehicles of the train are historic Maunsell-designed carriages largely dating from the 1930s. *Author*

Opposite bottom: Very, very occasionally railway photographers are blessed with almost unbelievable good luck and one such example is depicted here. The weather on 4th May 1998 was hardly conducive to photography with a blanket of slow-moving low cloud stretching as far as the eye could see in all directions but, just as the 3.55pm Kingscote to Sheffield Park train hove into view at Tremaines the sun suddenly, and totally unexpectedly, burst through a tiny gap in the clouds and No.80080 was momentarily bathed in glorious sunshine as it passed the photographer. Within seconds the sun, like the train, had gone and this picture bears ample testament to a truly 'magic moment'. *Author*

Yes, it is No.80080 again! This time the BR Standard 2-6-4T is seen passing a really eye-catching carpet of lineside bluebells as it passes Ketches Halt (out of view behind the train) with the 11.55am train *ex*-Kingscote on 13th May 1998. On the right of the picture is Sheffield Park's outer home signal. *David Cox*

The 6th/7th June 1998 were noteworthy for the running of some photographic charters. The one on the former date involved BR Standard 4-6-0s Nos.75027 and 73082 *Camelot* (masquerading as former sister engine No.73087 *Linette*) double-heading a re-creation of a Somerset & Dorset Railway express whilst the following day No.75027 was used on what was supposedly a goods train but, judging by its consist, the train would better be described as a civil engineers' dept. working. Anyway, No.75027 makes a splendid sight as it pulls away from Horsted Keynes in the sunshine. *Mike Esau*

The engine that came back from the dead. The Bluebell Railway is renowned for the extremely high standard of its repair and restoration work, exemplified here by this illustration of gleaming LBSCR E4 Class No.473 (better known as *Birch Grove*) posing outside Sheffield Park works on 12th June 1998 just after its release from the works. It should be noted that for a few weeks it carried 'LBSC' on the tanksides and painted numerals on the bunker, this being historically correct for a locomotive in Marsh umber livery. The E4 was used intensively in the 1960s/early 1970s and was completely worn out when it was withdrawn in late 1971. The restoration of the E4 actually began way back in 1983 when the boiler was lifted from the frames, and good progress was made with the repair in the mid-1980s, including extensive work on the firebox and frames. In 1988, however, work on the engine was suspended simply because other projects were more urgent and far less time consuming. In the early 1990s some Bluebell members voiced their concern that such a historic locomotive had been unserviceable for so long and a groundswell of opinion developed in favour of giving No.473 a much higher priority. Work resumed in determined fashion in 1995, 600 new boiler stays were fitted plus a new front tubeplate while yet more time was spent on the boiler. No.473's official return to steam took place on 20th June 1998, a day that will be long remembered by many Bluebell supporters. *John Scrace*

1999 There have been many very creditable preservation projects over the years at the Bluebell, but the restoration of LBSCR six-compartment first class carriage No.142 (SR No.7598) must surely rate as one of the greatest achievements of all. The coach, which was built at Brighton in 1903, had been used as part of a dwelling at West Chiltington following its withdrawal from traffic in 1931 and arrived at the Bluebell on 6th September 1989. The coach came without an underframe, but fortunately a suitable frame was located at Carnforth, Lancashire, and acquired by the No.7598 Coach Fund. When the carriage arrived it was basically a shell and most fittings were missing. Some replacement components were obtained from other grounded coach bodies, such as a complete LBSCR electric lighting system consisting of six glass bowls and matching Duplex twin bulb holders, obtained from a coach at Chichester. Other parts, for example blue leather door straps with white stitching, were specially manufactured, often in conjunction with other preserved railways. The seat backs and bases were made by a volunteer at Horsted Keynes, as were a multiplicity of other fittings, some of the smaller jobs being carried out by members at home. A huge amount of work was undertaken on the underframe, which had to be shortened to fit, while the bogies proved a particular headache when it was found necessary to replace all of the springs, an unwelcome and expensive discovery. A major milestone in the coach's overhaul occurred on 30th November 1994 when it was placed on its new underframe for the first time. After many years of painstaking, and often quite tedious and complex work, No.7598 made its unofficial debut in passenger service on 20th June 1998, albeit in unfinished condition, for the re-dedication of LBSCR No.473 *Birch Grove*. Its official entry into service on Bluebell metals occurred on 30th May 1999 and, almost needless to say, passengers marvelled at the excellent standard of workmanship. In 2002 the exceptional standard of the work involved in restoring No.7598 was officially recognised when the Heritage Railway Association selected it as 'the best coach of the year'. The splendidly restored vehicle is seen here posing for a portrait just south of Horsted Keynes station on 19th May 1999. *Mike Esau*

Almost ten years earlier, and having been used as an aviary, derelict coach No.7598 sits on a spare underframe at Horsted Keynes on 18th March 1990 awaiting restoration. *David Cox*

The Bluebell marked the centenary of the South Eastern & Chatham Railway by repainting No.323 *Bluebell* in SECR green livery, a colour scheme that was introduced just before the First World War by Maunsell as an economy measure. Apparently he considered the existing livery to be far too elaborate! The newly repainted locomotive, which was quickly dubbed *Greenbell* by enginemen, is seen at Horsted Keynes on 21st June 1999. A major project in full swing at that time was the reinstatement of the buildings and canopy on Platforms One and Two at Horsted Keynes which had been swept away by the LBSCR at the time of the First World War. The new structures totally transformed the bare, uninviting westernmost platforms and restored the balance and homogeneity of the station that had been lost all of those years ago. New buildings on that side of the premises now provide a popular venue for weddings and other functions, whilst one of the rooms is being used (at the time of writing) to house the Railway's museum. The latter is a temporary arrangement as a result of building work at Sheffield Park station. *Matthew Cousins*

One of the most interesting visitors to the Bluebell was veteran North British Railway Class J36 0-6-0 No.65243 *Maude,* owned by the Scottish Railway Preservation Society, which came down from its home at Bo'ness, on the firth of Forth, to star in 'The Railway Children'. The making of this film not only proved quite lucrative for the Railway but also provided much valuable publicity. *Maude* arrived on the Bluebell on 7th October 1999 and subsequently spent a month on the line for filming purposes. Unfortunately, it was deemed by the Bluebell's locomotive staff to be a trifle too delicate to use on passenger services and consequently it saw very little use. Judging by the paucity of pictures submitted for this album, photographing No.65243 proved something of a challenge for photographers, because it usually worked spasmodically during the week and not at weekends. *Maude* is depicted at Horsted Keynes whilst preparing stock for a filming session. *Ian Wright*

2000 Pictured in brilliant early morning sunshine, Bulleid Q1 Class 0-6-0 No.33001 (alias Southern Railway No.C1) emits a worthwhile smoke effect for the benefit of photographers while powering a charter train comprised of civil engineers' dept wagons. The Q1 was photographed passing beneath Three Arch Bridge, just south of Horsted Keynes, on 7th May 2000. The distinctive Q1 Class locomotive, which had been on loan to the Bluebell from the National Railway Museum since the mid-1970s, returned 'home' to York in May 2004. *Roger Cruse*

The 28th December 2000 was one of those really memorable winter days when everything was 'just right' for the railway photographer. There was a reasonable dusting of snow on the fields, the sun shone strongly all day long and, most importantly, there was absolutely no breeze which could have blown down exhaust smoke from a locomotive and ruined a picture just at the crucial moment. Here, the shadows are lengthening as LBSCR 0-6-2T No.473 *Birch Grove* passes Tremaines with a northbound train in rapidly fading light at the end of a day that will be forever etched in the memory. The year 2000 was a noteworthy one in the history of the Bluebell on many different fronts. That year saw the last piece of land purchased for the extension to East Grinstead, while Sheffield Park station was almost cut off by some of the worst flooding in living memory when the river Ouse burst its banks. On the locomotive side, three visiting 'Terriers' helped *Stepney* celebrate its 125th birthday, the Maunsell Locomotive Society purchased 'Schools' Class engine No.928 *Stowe* and *Blackmore Vale* returned to traffic after a long lay-off. So it was quite a year! *Author*

2001 The return to traffic of No.672 *Fenchurch* took place on 10th February 2001, a dreary and damp day that perpetuated *Fenchurch*'s reputation as the 'rainmaker'. It was restored in Marsh umber livery in a new guise as an A1 Class locomotive. The following weekend it took centre stage at the Bluebell's annual 'Branch Line Weekend' on 17th/18th February and is seen here, piloted by visiting 'Terrier' No.8 *Freshwater,* darting out from beneath a farm occupation bridge at Holywell with the 1.08pm Horsted Keynes to Sheffield Park train: both locomotives are polished to perfection. The coach formed immediately behind the locomotive is the LNWR observation car which was running temporarily in LMSR crimson lake livery. *John Scrace*

The unique and extremely distinctive design of Bulleid's Pacifics has ensured a huge following among the railway enthusiast fraternity and it can be said that, for admirers of these engines, if anything is better than one Bulleid Pacific at the head of a train it is two! This was realised at the Bluebell Railway on 20th July 2001 when visiting locomotive No.34081 *92 Squadron* teamed up with Bulleid Society-owned No.21C123 *Blackmore Vale* and the pair are seen here entering Horsted Keynes with a photographers' special train, this being the first time two 'Bulleids' double-headed on the Bluebell. Note that the leading engine is in Southern Railway livery, but carries BR numbering and lettering. The train comprises mostly matching Bulleid coaches apart from one BR Standard Mk1 vehicle towards the rear. *Roger Cruse*

Those enthusiasts who like to see the Bluebell's most powerful locomotives hauling heavy trains to an intensive timetable always enjoy the run-up to Christmas. The month of December has become one of the busiest (not to mention most lucrative) periods in the railway's calendar and the usually cold conditions can produce sparkling pictures, provided the sun is shining, of course. In this shot the mighty BR Standard Class 9F 2-10-0 No.92240 disturbs the peace of the Sussex countryside near Vaux End as it blasts upgrade towards West Hoathly tunnel with a 'Santa Special' in December 2001. This is a particularly lonely stretch of line with only a few farmhouses in the vicinity so the sound of trains pulling away from Horsted Keynes station, about a mile distant, is interrupted only by the noise of farm animals or aircraft heading for Gatwick Airport – what a diabolical intrusion! *Author*

2002 New Year's Day 2002 dawned with bitterly cold conditions after a very heavy overnight frost and the majority of the population were doubtless still in bed nursing hangovers when the Bluebell's first train of the new year left Sheffield Park station. Here it is depicted approaching Horsted House farm crossing with Nos.55 *Stepney* and 672 *Fenchurch* in charge of a mixed formation consisting of the LBSCR six-compartment first coach No.7598, immediately behind the locomotives, followed by the two Metropolitan Railway carriages that were operational at that time and the LNWR observation car. The two veteran 'Terriers', which had an amazing combined age of 255 years when the picture was taken, emit a huge pall of smoke and steam which hangs in the cold, still air as they approach the camera. The photographer's brave decision to get out of bed on an icy morning and drive along to the Bluebell was amply rewarded. Wonderful! *Tony Eaton*

The author has always wondered why the Bluebell has never had a visit by a LMSR Stanier Class 5MT 4-6-0 which (at least in his expert opinion!) are by far the most reliable, versatile and economical main line engines ever built in Great Britain, 842 examples being constructed over a period of sixteen years. What better commendation could there be? At least compensation is provided by the presence of the next best thing, so to speak, BR Standard Class 5MT No.73082 *Camelot,* which is seen here hauling a set of maroon coaches past Holywell waterworks during a period of brilliant late afternoon sunshine on 2nd March 2002. *Roger Cruse*

A true giant of steam. The Bluebell Railway is fortunate to have BR Standard Class 9F No.92240 in its collection, a representative of a class that is widely considered to have been the most successful of the BR Standard types. The Class 9F worked regularly on the Bluebell from September 1990 until it was withdrawn for overhaul on 21st November 2002. The locomotive, naturally, played its part in the annual 'Giants of Steam' weekend in October and was then given a final chance to stretch its legs on a charter goods working prior to being taken out of traffic. This special train, which was organised by the Severn Valley Railway Association/Battle of Britain Locomotive Society, ran on 4th November 2002 and in this portrait No.92240 is seen rounding the curve near the site of Freshfield Halt with a reasonable rake of goods vehicles in tow, but this was hardly a stern test of the phenomenal haulage capacity of these excellent machines. No.92240 was actually an opportune substitute at short notice for Bulleid Pacific No.34027 *Taw Valley,* on loan from the Severn Valley Railway, which had been declared unfit. A major event during 2002 was the visit of HRH Princess Alexandra which took place on 17th July as part of a tour of various establishments in East Sussex. It was the first royal visit to the Bluebell Railway. The Princess unveiled a commemorative plaque in the booking hall at Sheffield Park before meeting 'Golden Arrow' staff and taking lunch on the train. *David Cox*

2003 Kingscote as it is today, beautifully restored and lovingly maintained – a real gem of a station if ever there was one. Public car parking is not permitted at Kingscote and passengers wishing to start their journey there must arrive by public transport, cycle or on foot. The station has consequently retained much of the quiet rural charm of a bygone era where the unhurried atmosphere of a branch line station can still be experienced. The train featured in this shot is particularly appropriate to the Bluebell, the LMSR Ivatt-designed Class 2MT tank locomotives, had worked along Bluebell metals until the line was closed in 1958, and many members wanted to recreate some classic 1950s scenes using No.41312, which was based not far away on the Mid Hants Railway. It was hoped that the locomotive would be able to appear at the Bluebell's traditional 'Branch Line Weekend' event on 22nd/23rd February 2003, but unfortunately the Bluebell's finances were stretched at that quiet time of year and it was clear that the Ivatt would be unlikely to appear owing to the prohibitive cost of road movement. A member of the Bluebell's locomotive department liaised with some charter organisers, however, and established that there was considerable interest from the photographic fraternity and their financial support would enable the Ivatt engine to visit the Bluebell. The Ivatt arrived on 11th February and was unloaded facing southwards, which opened up a range of possibilities for the photographic brigade on a line where most engines face northwards. Here, No.41312 runs through Kingscote station with a charter train, thus magically recreating an everyday scene from the 1950s. This shot was taken on a bright 17th February 2003. *David Cox*

Inset: Kingscote station, idyllically situated at the top of a secluded valley near Gravetye Woods, unexpectedly came onto the market in the summer of 1984 and the Bluebell secured the property for £102,000. The structure had suffered ill-conceived alterations since closure and there was extensive rot, but despite these formidable problems a party of committed and determined Bluebell members started the lengthy process of restoring the station to its former glory in January 1985, and within two years the premises had regained much of its old character. When this picture of Kingscote station was taken in early 1994 track laying was in progress from New Coombe bridge and the first public passenger train arrived on 23rd April 1994 with the 'official' reopening taking place a month later. *Graham Mallinson*

Displaying headcode discs that indicate an Oxted to Brighton via East Grinstead (Low Level) train, Ivatt Class 2MT No.41312 waits at Horsted Keynes station during a photographic charter on 20th February 2003. In order to recreate a scene from the mid-1950s, the 'Mickey Mouse' tank locomotive had been disguised as No.41319, a locomotive that was based at Tunbridge Wells West shed during that period and regularly worked over the former East Grinstead to Lewes line. In addition, to make the illusion even more convincing, it is also displaying locomotive duty number 668 which, in the mid-1950s, was carried by engines working over the line. In 1955, shortly before the first closure of the route, this duty apparently covered the 2.34pm East Grinstead to Brighton train and 5.18pm Brighton to Victoria via East Grinstead. So, the organisers obviously had an eye for detail.
Rodney Lissenden

Sir Nigel Gresley's V2 Class 2-6-2s were constructed over an eight year period from June 1936 to July 1944, 184 examples being built in total. They have sometimes been described as 'the engines that helped win the war' due to their prodigious haulage capacity which kept traffic moving along the East Coast main line under difficult wartime conditions. The doyen of the class, No.60800 *Green Arrow,* was fortunately scheduled for preservation when it was withdrawn in August 1962 and the Bluebell obtained the locomotive on loan for a three-week spell in the autumn of 2003, which included the 'Giants of Steam' weekend. Fifty years earlier Class V2s had worked on the Southern for a short time, deputising for Bulleid Pacifics that had to be temporarily withdrawn from traffic after a serious incident, so the timing of the visit was highly appropriate. These three-cylinder locomotives had a very distinctive staccato-like exhaust beat and there is no doubt that No.60800 proved to be a very popular performer during its stint on the Bluebell. Here, *Green Arrow,* with the GNR Directors' saloon marshalled immediately behind the engine, tackles the 1 in 75 climb up to Horsted Keynes station in typically energetic style – what a shame the engine's stay at the Bluebell was so brief. *Author*

2004 Strangely, despite providing a wonderful grandstand for photographers, this is the only picture taken from the footbridge at Sheffield Park submitted for publication. Perhaps photographers are deterred by the constant flow of people using the bridge or perhaps because few Bluebell locomotives face southwards. Here, on 7th February 2004, No.672 *Fenchurch* simmers in the down platform at the head of the 'Chesham' set as a northbound train gets underway from the other platform. It should be noted that the 'Chesham' set was formed of only three vehicles at that time, the fourth coach still being under restoration. The canopy visible on the extreme right is part of the Bluebell shop which has since been demolished, so this picture is now of considerable historical interest. *Rodney Lissenden*

Following the visit of *Green Arrow* in October 2003 the Bluebell must have obtained a liking for noisy three-cylinder locomotives, because the guest engine at the 2004 'Giants of Steam' event was LMSR-designed 'Jubilee' 4-6-0 No.5690 *Leander*. One of a class of 191, No.5690 was built at Crewe in March 1936 and based at Bristol (Barrow Road) shed for many years for hauling expresses on the cross-country route to the Midlands and north of England. It was secured for preservation following withdrawal and is a regular performer on main line enthusiasts' specials. In addition to working during the 'Giants of Steam' weekend No.5690 also put in an appearance during the Bluebell's 'Wizard Weekend' a week later, and is seen here on 31st October charging up Freshfield bank leaving a spectacular pall of smoke across the Sussex countryside. The year 2004 was especially noteworthy because the Heritage Lottery Fund announced a grant of £2,935,000 towards Operation Undercover, a scheme to provide much-needed covered accommodation for the bulk of the Railway's historic carriage fleet. *David Clark*

2005

The year 2005 finally saw what many photographers had for years been clamouring for, namely the repainting of LBSCR E4 Class 0-6-2T No.473 *Birch Grove* in BR black livery. The E4s worked over the line for many years so the repainting provided the opportunity for many past scenes to be recreated. It was originally intended that its appearance in BR colours would be brief before the engine was repainted in early Southern green livery, but the anticipated sponsorship for this was not forthcoming and, in any case, it is doubtful whether the hard-pressed Sheffield Park locomotive works would have had the capacity to carry out the repainting. In the event, and much to the approval of many enthusiasts, the E4 continued in BR livery until the expiration of its boiler certificate in May 2008. This photograph was taken near Horsted House Farm during a photographic charter on 22nd February 2005 when there was a light sprinkling of snow on the ground to add even more interest to the picture. *Graham Mallinson*

The E4 Class engine may have achieved a degree of stardom in its 'new' livery, but it still had to earn its keep as a member of the Bluebell's operational locomotive fleet, and in this illustration it is seen on a much more mundane and low profile duty working a spoil train at Imberhorne Lane on 20th June 2005. Since work began to remove the rubbish tip that (at the time of writing) blocks the Bluebell's way to East Grinstead, a variety of locomotives has worked these trains, including Ivatt Class 2MT 2-6-2T No.41312, which was on extended loan for a considerable period, and 350hp diesel shunters that were hired primarily for shunting but also powered many of the spoil trains. The acquisition on loan of the latter angered many die-hard steam enthusiasts among the Railway's membership, but it has to be said that the shunters, which are 'ready to go' instantly at the flick of a switch, proved to be a very effective substitute for steam and certainly a more economical one. *Ian Wright*

There is no doubt that the steam railway at night time really stirs the imagination. There is the crimson glow from the fire 'dancing' on the engine's exhaust, the rhythmic clanks from the motion as the locomotive passes by largely unseen and the occasional spark from the chimney. No.35005 *Canadian Pacific* was visiting the Bluebell from the Mid Hants Railway and was utilized for a photographic charter, which included an after-dark session at Horsted Keynes. *Canadian Pacific* was withdrawn from BR service in October 1965 and was sent to Barry scrap yard where it lay until purchased in March 1973. After restoration the engine controversially ran in blue livery for a time, recalling the days when locomotives of this class ran in this colour during the late 1940s/early 1950s. It was restored to green livery during a repaint in early 2001 but is out of traffic at the time of writing after the expiry of its boiler certificate. Photographed on a very wet night in October 1964, Bulleid 'Merchant Navy' Class 8P Pacific No.35005 *Canadian Pacific*, of Weymouth shed, waits to leave Southampton Central with the 5.35pm Weymouth to Waterloo train which included a restaurant car. Well, that is possibly the kind of picture some of the gathered multitude of photographers were trying to recreate during a session at Horsted Keynes on 22nd October 2005 when this shot was taken. *Mike Esau*

2006 After the storm. Jet black clouds still hover menacingly over Rock Cutting, near Tremaines, after a thunderstorm but the sun has just broken through and beautifully illuminates BR Standard Class 4MT No.75027 as it passes by with the 3.00pm Sheffield Park to Kingscote train on 14th April 2006. The photographer, who is a Bluebell working member engaged on permanent way duties, comments that he often takes his camera when on track work but usually there is no reason to take it out of its bag. On this occasion some of the permanent way gang had got soaked earlier in the day and spent most of the afternoon sheltering in a lineside hut. *Jon Bowers*

The Bluebell was host to three visiting LBSCR 'Terriers' during a four-day 'Terrier weekend' between the 10th and 13th of November 2006. Both of the Bluebell's own locomotives, *Fenchurch* and *Stepney,* were available for traffic so the Railway had no fewer than five of these magnificent little beasts puffing and panting up and down the line – wonderful! It had originally been hoped that six engines would be available to entertain the masses; unfortunately, the Kent & East Sussex Railway lost its battle to have No.3 *Bodiam* ready in time, but at least that railway was represented by No.32678. The following day this locomotive 'assisted' BR Standard tank locomotive No.80151 (running as No.80154) on the 12.45pm train from Sheffield Park – what a remarkable combination. The other visitors were No.8 *Freshwater,* from the Isle of Wight Steam Railway, and No.662 from the Bressingham Steam Museum in East Anglia. The Bluebell operating staff had to be extra careful because the former is fitted only with air brakes and could not be used single-headed on vacuum-braked passenger trains, but short goods trains, such as this one seen here on Freshfield bank on 10th November, presented no problem. The 'Terrier' gathering ended on the Monday with all five engines in steam and positioned for photography at Horsted Keynes. *Roger Cruse*

The National Railway Museum-owned 'City' Class 4-4-0 No.3440 *City of Truro* paid a visit to the Bluebell Railway in October 2006 and this enabled the locomotive to be paired with the Bluebell's resident 'Dukedog' No.9017 *Earl of Berkeley*. Here, the two surviving outside-framed 4-4-0s are seen posing for photographers during an evening photo-shoot at Sheffield Park station on 15th October 2006. Built in 1903, No.3440 was withdrawn in 1931 and subsequently spent many years incarcerated, somewhat inappropriately, in York Museum surrounded by mostly LNER, and its constituent companies' engines. What a way to treat a famous Great Western locomotive but, in fairness, it has to be said that at the time no other suitable 'home' was available! Salvation came, however, in 1957 when sanity prevailed and No.3440 was overhauled and returned to capital stock for use on rail tours and other special trains. It even appeared regularly on timetabled services in the Didcot and Swindon area and the author can just remember the excitement a gleaming No.3440 caused when it worked into Eastleigh, presumably with a train from Didcot. Surely, the classic lines of *City of Truro* take some beating? *Jon Bowers*

A new angle on Freshfield bank. Many thousands of photographs have been taken of trains climbing Freshfield bank from the traditional positions in fields adjoining the line but, for a change, here is a picture taken from a different viewpoint. This scene was photographed from high ground to the west of the line and depicts BR Standard Class 4MT 4-6-0 No.75027 ascending the bank with the 1.00pm Sheffield Park to Horsted Keynes train on 19th November 2006. No.75027 was overhauled in the Bluebell's workshops in the mid-1990s and entered service after its latest repair in October 1997, so by the date of this picture it was nearing the end of its boiler certificate after over nine years' yeoman service. *Jon Bowers*

2007 A highly appropriate pairing. The Metropolitan Railway E Class 0-4-4T No.1, which is kept at the Buckinghamshire Railway Centre, Quainton Road, near Aylesbury, paid a visit to the Bluebell in the summer of 2007 and paraded up and down for the benefit of photographers, hauling the 'Chesham' set of carriages. The set had just been made up to its full complement of four coaches after the completion of the final vehicle. It is depicted in this illustration making a false start from Horsted Keynes station on the glorious evening of 29th July 2007. *Ian Wright*

A stunning night-time portrait of Nos. 34007 *Wadebridge* and No.34081 92 *Squadron* at the north end of Horsted Keynes station on 30th October 2007. No.34007 was restored at the Bodmin and Wenford Railway while the restoration of No.34081 was undertaken at the Nene Valley Railway, near Peterborough. The former locomotive is the oldest Bulleid Light Pacific in preservation having been out-shopped from Brighton works in September 1945, whilst No.34081 entered traffic exactly three years later. *Wadebridge* spent much of its career at Nine Elms shed in south London while 92 *Squadron* worked on the South Eastern Section from Ramsgate shed before being moved to Exmouth Junction. *Mike Esau*

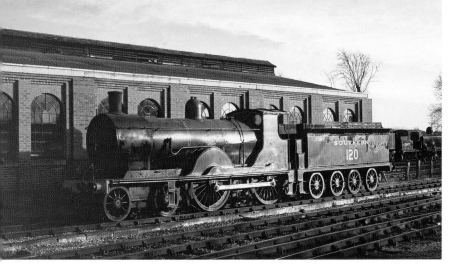

2008 Surely, one of the most elegant classes of locomotive ever to grace Bluebell tracks is the LSWR T9 Class 4-4-0. The National Railway Museum's No.120 (BR No.30120) was photographed at Sheffield Park, with the impressive wall of the engine shed as a backdrop, on 12th January 2008 just before it left for pastures new at the Bodmin & Wenford Railway. Amazingly, the T9 had spent almost fourteen years at Sheffield Park during which time it never turned a wheel under its own steam. There always seemed to be more deserving cases in the locomotive repair queue and the fact that the locomotive was not owned by the Bluebell further complicated the issue. A restoration fund was started by a Bluebell member but, sadly, this failed to get off the ground. Designed by Dugald Drummond, sixty-six of these machines were built between 1899 and 1901, construction being shared between the LSWR's Nine Elms works and Dubs & Co., No.120 being one of the first batch out-shopped in August 1899. Due to their free-running capabilities the engines were nicknamed 'Greyhounds'. They were built for express passenger work but as trains became heavier they were ousted by larger, more powerful machines. No.120 spent long periods working from Fratton and Eastleigh sheds and earned a place in the history books when it powered the final passenger working from Newbury to Eastleigh on 5th March 1960. After withdrawal in June 1961 No.120 was restored for use on enthusiasts' specials and re-entered traffic in March 1962. On final 'official' withdrawal in July 1963 (it actually worked two rail tours after its withdrawal) it became part of the National Collection and some years later ran for a time on the Mid Hants and Swanage Railways, before coming to the Bluebell in 1994. The western wall of the locomotive running shed cost around £75,000 to construct, of which two-thirds was raised by a fund organised by volunteers, the remainder being met by the Bluebell Trust. The finishing touches were applied on 2nd February 2006 when the last of 720 panes of glass were fitted to the large arched windows. No job is ever easy at the Bluebell! *Ian Wright*

Very occasionally new photographic opportunities are created by farmers who own land adjacent to the Bluebell, an example being this pond that has been enlarged in recent years. It is located on the western side of Freshfield bank and enables a reflection of passing trains to be obtained. Here GWR 0-4-2T No.1450 propels its one-coach train up the bank on a sunny 10th February 2008. *Tony Eaton*

A classic Great Western pairing. Class 1400 0-4-2T No.1450 and its matching auto coach No.178 visited the Bluebell for a spell during early 2008 as a special attraction at the 'Branch Line Weekend' on 23rd/24th February. Constructed at Swindon Works, No.1450 was out-shopped in July 1935 and lasted in traffic until May 1965 when it was one of the last two engines of its class to be withdrawn. Shortly before withdrawal No.1450 made a notable appearance on a former Southern Railway branch line when it was commandeered to work on the Seaton branch for a brief period in early 1965 as a result of the Exeter District being desperately short of diesel units. It should, perhaps, be mentioned that the Western Region had taken over all lines west of Salisbury by that time, hence the appearance of a WR train! The visit of the auto train to the Bluebell proved very popular and most trains were well patronised. In this illustration it is seen leaving Kingscote in glorious afternoon sunshine on 17th February 2008, doubtless with another load of happy customers in tow. *John Scrace*

Maunsell 'Mogul' No.1638 – mission impossible. A huge mass of dark cloud hovers overhead, but the sun breaks through just at the right moment as Maunsell 'Mogul' No.1638 pulls away from Horsted Keynes station with a goods charter train on 28th March 2008. The locomotive was bought from Barry scrap yard by a Bluebell member and was the 114th to leave the yard: it arrived on the Bluebell on 30th July 1980. The Bluebell offered the engine to the Maunsell Society on a fifty-year lease with the proviso that it was restored for use on the line. There were many doubters who thought its restoration was not feasible, but they had not reckoned with the sheer determination and dedication of the Maunsell Society who, backed by the enthusiastic support of the Bluebell, commenced work in earnest in May 1993 when the boiler was separated from the engine's

frame. Many man-hours were expended on the tender, which was newly constructed using the frames of a 'Schools' Class locomotive's tender that BR had converted to a snowplough. It was a real stroke of luck that a suitable tender frame was available, albeit in considerably modified condition. After substantial expenditure on the locomotive No.1638 was steam tested on 2nd February 2006 and officially returned to service at a joint Bluebell/ Maunsell Society ceremony on 18th February. The cold, miserable weather could not dampen the spirits of those present, many of whom had contributed in some way to what many regard as a preservation miracle. Mission accomplished! *David Cox*

Without a doubt, by far the best-known locomotive on the Bluebell is the diminutive LBSCR 'Terrier' Class A1X 0-6-0T No.55 *Stepney* which was made famous in the Rev. Awdry's series of classic children's books. Built at Brighton in 1875, *Stepney* was the Bluebell's first locomotive and it has been a favourite with visitors ever since it arrived at the railway in May 1960. Unfortunately, owing to a limited traffic requirement for small engines, *Stepney*, despite being the line's flagship locomotive, has spent much time out of service and after another of these dormant periods during the early 1990s it was decided to overhaul the 'Terrier', this having the added advantage that it would be in traffic on its 125th birthday in November 2000. Work started in late 1997, the repair involving the manufacture of a new front tubeplate and smokebox, and this iconic Bluebell locomotive was returned to service on 4th July 1998. Shortly before its boiler insurance expired in May 2008 No.55 operated a series of 'Farewell to Stepney' trains for its many fans and here *Stepney* is seen emerging from West Hoathly tunnel with a farewell special on 9th April 2008. Sadly, by this date No.55 was extremely frail and probably incapable of hauling a heavier train than that seen here. At the time of writing *Stepney* is undergoing a further repair which should ensure its participation in the Bluebell's 50th anniversary celebrations, and there are certainly many people who can't wait for the return of this celebrity machine. *Tony Eaton*

A disproportionately large number of slides taken in 2008 were submitted for publication in this album, reflecting a year full of interesting events even by the Bluebell's standards. In this masterpiece of a picture SECR O1 Class No.65 pilots C Class No.592 up Freshfield bank with an early morning goods charter train on 13th September 2008. The idea was to obtain some rare shots in sun on the eastern side of the line, but the plan seemed to have been thwarted by the weather when the participants gathered just before 7.00am to find themselves surrounded by dense fog. However, the sun started to burn off the fog just in time and the two locomotives made a truly evocative and memorable sight as they plodded up the 1 in 75 gradient. *Jon Bowers*

Opposite top: Photographed on 26th April 2008, No.21C123 *Blackmore Vale* hauls the 10.32am Sheffield Park to Horsted Keynes empty stock train up the 1 in 75 gradient at the approach to Three Arch bridge. The Pullman carriages were being worked northwards to form a wedding special later that morning. Sadly, less than two months after this shot was taken No.21C123 was diagnosed with severe wastage of its firebox and had to be withdrawn from service prematurely. This was a cruel blow to the locomotive department, and the Bluebell generally, who had expected to retain the services of *Blackmore Vale* until the expiration of its boiler certificate in 2010. The Bluebell suffered another setback to the locomotive fleet later in the year when the Maunsell Society's invaluable 'Mogul' No.1638 had to be taken out of traffic. Such are the vicissitudes of running the railway with museum pieces! *John Scrace*

Opposite bottom: Much to the delight of many enthusiasts, the LBSCR E4 Class locomotive No.32473 stayed at work in BR black livery until its boiler certificate expired in May 2008. Consequently it was booked to work a number of charter trains for photographers and in this portrait No.32473 is seen leaving West Hoathly tunnel with one of these trains on 28th April 2008, just over a week before it was withdrawn. The line is falling at 1 in 75 at this point, so a shot with 'steam on' is normally only obtainable on a charter working. The coaches forming the train are two (then) recently acquired Mk1 vehicles plus a Bulleid brake coach. The coach nearest to the camera is First Open (FO) No.3064 which was purchased for use on the Bluebell's new Lounge Car service while the other vehicle is a 48-seater Second Open, No.4824, which has particularly spacious seating, and can be used as a first or second class vehicle as required. *Jon Bowers*

The official launch of the excavation of Imberhorne tip took place on 25th November 2008, guests being conveyed in a special train from Sheffield Park to the (then) limit of operations near Imberhorne Lane bridge. A short platform was constructed to enable them to safely alight from the train. The mayor of East Grinstead, Councillor Ginnie Waddingham, and TV presenter Nick Owen set the giant excavator to work on clearing the cutting, which is 500 metres long and up to 12 metres deep. The ceremony was performed in the presence of other local dignitaries, officers of the Bluebell Railway and representatives of the contractors. The train, which was propelled up to the bridge from Kingscote by SECR O1 Class 0-6-0 No.65, was formed of two Mk1 coaches including First Class Lounge Car No.3064. Note the flat bottom rails on concrete sleepers! *Graham Mallinson*

A view of Imberhorne Lane bridge taken on the same day as the previous shot. Prior to the start of excavation the top of the tip reached to just below the parapet of the bridge, so this gives some idea of the size of the tip and the enormity of the task facing the Bluebell. But the Railway has successfully overcome seemingly insuperable obstacles in the past and many people thought that Bluebell tracks would never reach Kingscote. Here's hoping! *Graham Mallinson*

'Welcome home, No.80151'. It is not often that the Bluebell is offered a complete locomotive in almost 'ready to run' condition, but that is what happened in 1998 when the railway was approached by the owners of BR Standard Class 4MT 2-6-4T No.80151. The engine had been under repair at the East Anglian Railway Museum, Essex, and was in an advanced state of restoration when it arrived at Sheffield Park on long-term loan on 3rd July 1998. Members of the 80151 Locomotive Co. were present when, on 11th October 2001, it was steamed for the first time in thirty-four years. The locomotive, which was built at Brighton works in January 1957, was based at Brighton shed for much of its short working life, so it really was a case of 'welcome home'. On 20th October, No.80151, looking absolutely resplendent after the completion of its comprehensive overhaul at Sheffield Park, worked a special train for the owning group and entered ordinary service at the end of October, becoming the third member of the class to work on Bluebell metals. Needless to say, No.80151 is a very powerful locomotive and capable of hauling the heaviest Bluebell trains as depicted in this illustration, which shows the Standard tank running downhill under Three Arch Bridge, south of Horsted Keynes, with a 'Santa Special' working on 7th December 2008. Engines would not usually have steam on at this point, but sometimes Bluebell drivers are sympathetic to the requirements of lineside cameramen! *Tony Eaton*

In the spring of 2008 Great Western Railway 5100 Class 2-6-2T No.5199 was hired from the 5199 Project and arrived from the Llangollen Railway, where it is based, on 24th April 2008. It was too wide for Platform Nos.4 and 5 at Horsted Keynes, so it always had to be routed into Platform Nos.2 and 3. Unfortunately, the summer of 2008 proved to be a difficult one for the locomotive department, as previously mentioned: the enforced withdrawal of *Blackmore Vale* in June was bad enough but this was followed by the discovery that 148 firebox stays needed replacing on Maunsell 'Mogul' No.1638. This necessitated a boiler lift and the temporary withdrawal of this highly useful locomotive during the busy Christmas season, just when its services were most needed. Consequently, No.5199, ably supported by former Somerset and Dorset 2-8-0 No.53809 on loan from the Midland Railway Centre, Butterley, handled most of the Christmas traffic. In this portrait No.5199 is seen leaving Sheffield Park with great gusto with one of these workings on 7th December 2008. *Author*

The Bluebell's 2008 Christmas trains were largely handled, as mentioned in the previous caption, by two visiting locomotives, this being a result of the chronic motive power shortage affecting the Railway at that time. In this shot an afternoon working, hauled by Somerset & Dorset 7F Class 2-8-0 No.53809, which is emitting a volcanic smoke effect, comes up the 1 in 75 gradient towards Horsted Keynes station and is beautifully illuminated by the soft, afternoon winter sunshine. No.53809's load is a mere six coaches, and it is worth remembering that in BR days, when these machines worked heavy summer holiday trains over the Somerset & Dorset line, they were permitted to take ten carriages over the route's 1 in 50 gradients without assistance – two more than BR Standard Class 5MTs or Bulleid Pacifics – so it is unlikely that No.53809 was unduly taxed by its load on this occasion! This picture was also taken on 7th December 2008. Many enthusiasts undoubtedly enjoyed seeing No.53809 charging up and down the line, but for many members by far the most significant event during the year was the start of operations to remove the huge rubbish tip blocking the way to East Grinstead, the work being mainly financed by an appeal to members and well-wishers. Unfortunately, the launch of the appeal coincided with an international financial crisis and, whilst a very creditable total was raised, at the time of writing a considerable amount still needs to be found before success can be guaranteed. *Author*

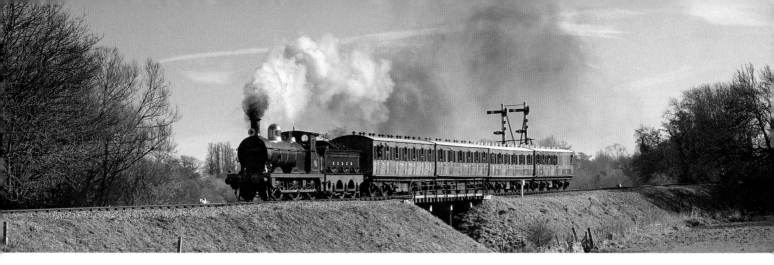

2009

The SECR O1 Class 0-6-0 No.65 (BR No.31065) was rescued for preservation by a private individual at the last minute when awaiting cutting-up at Ashford in early 1963. Originally built as an O Class at Ashford in 1896, it was rebuilt by Wainwright in 1908 and re-designated O1. The class had outside-framed tenders and looked especially archaic, but nonetheless No.31065 lasted sixty-six years in service, its very light axle loading, which enabled it to be used on lightly laid tracks, being a factor in its longevity. It was withdrawn by BR in June 1961 a few days after its finest hour powering, together with SECR C Class No.31592, an enthusiasts' special from Paddock Wood to Hawkhurst and back to Tonbridge. No.65 was displayed for some years at the South Eastern Steam Centre, Ashford, but when that attraction closed its future was in some doubt and components of No.65 were spirited away to various 'secret' far-flung locations such as Sellindge, Kent, and Gamlingay in Cambridgeshire. It had been the intention to start restoration but, in reality, very little work was undertaken, apart from removal of the boiler tubes, and the engine became one of preservation's forgotten locomotives. In the late 1990s, however, its owner paid a visit to the Bluebell, and was impressed by the repair facilities available at Sheffield Park and the high standards achieved. He became receptive to a proposal to move No.65 to the Bluebell with the objective of restoring it in time for the centenary of the formation of the SECR in 1999. Preservation's 'lost' engine returned from oblivion on 29th July 1999 when it was given a test run after a comprehensive overhaul at Sheffield Park and, very much in the limelight for a change, worked its first passenger train for many years on 5th August. Here it is seen pulling away from Sheffield Park with the 'Chesham' set in tow on 21st February 2009 during the Railway's 'Branch Line Weekend'. The magnificent restoration of the 'Chesham' set, another Bluebell preservation miracle, was officially recognised when it won the Heritage Railway Association's Carriage & Wagon competition in 2006. *John Scrace*

Another shot at the same location on the same day. The Kent & East Sussex Railway loaned SECR P Class 0-6-0T No.753 for a short period in early 2009 and it was the star attraction at the Bluebell's annual 'Branch Line Weekend'. No.753 is perhaps better known to some enthusiasts as BR No.31556, the locomotive that survived in industrial use for shunting the flour mill at Robertsbridge. Sussex is hardly noted for engines in industrial service so No.753 has a genuine claim to fame. It is pictured leaving Sheffield Park, bathed in glorious winter sunshine, on 21st February with a delightful mixed train in tow comprising two vintage four-wheeled coaches plus an assortment of superbly restored goods vehicles. The coach immediately behind the locomotive is London, Chatham & Dover Railway brake third No.114, while the second vehicle is LBSCR Stroudley coach No.661: the latter was highly commended in the Heritage Railway Association's 2004 carriage and wagon competition. Once upon a time there was always at least one P Class engine serviceable at the Bluebell, but in recent years engines of this class have been conspicuous by their absence, so the visit of No.753 revived a few memories! Fans of these sturdy little engines will no doubt be pleased to hear that (at the time of writing) No.178 is nearing the end of a painstaking, thorough overhaul and may have entered traffic by the time this book is published. An overhaul is also currently underway on No.323 *Bluebell* with a view to returning this engine to service during the Railway's fiftieth anniversary year. *John Scrace*

Perhaps one of the most controversial decisions ever taken by the Bluebell management was that to accept on loan for a two-month period in early 2009 former BR Class 73/1 electro-diesel locomotive No.73 136 *Perseverance,* which is better known perhaps as No.E6043. The purpose of the locomotive's visit was to substitute for the Class 08 diesel shunter on spoil train duties. Some die-hard steam enthusiasts among the Bluebell's membership, who doubtless treasure the line's 'steam only' passenger operation, were angered by the decision, whilst others probably took the view that a small diesel fleet at Sheffield Park might attract younger members. In the event nobody tied themselves to the track in protest or jumped off the Ouse bridge, nor were there mass resignations among the membership. Those opposed to the visit were doubtless further antagonised when it was announced that No.73 136 was to work a special passenger train to raise funds for the extension, the Bluebell's first ever diesel-hauled train. Despite the premium fare charged the historic special was reasonably well patronised and it is seen here passing Horsted Keynes on 7th March 2009. *Graham Mallinson*

A spoil train heading for Horsted Keynes with No.73 136 in charge passes Vaux End in glorious afternoon sunshine on 11th March 2009. The employment of the electro-diesel locomotive may not have met with universal approval, but at least it was an out-of-the-ordinary subject for photographers and one, unlike steam locomotives(!), that was always the 'right way round'. One wonders how long it will be before a similar locomotive is seen again on Bluebell tracks. *Graham Mallinson*

The culmination of thirty years' endeavour. Bulleid 'Battle of Britain' Class Pacific No.34059 *Sir Archibald Sinclair* eases out of Sheffield Park station and begins the climb of Freshfield bank with a 300 Club members' special on 21st April 2009. No.34059 arrived at the Bluebell from Barry on 27th October 1979 following months of frantic fund raising among Bluebell supporters. It was very much a race against time because the price of metal on the world's markets was rising steadily and the scrap value of the engine was increasing all the time. The locomotive was purchased for £7,250, of which £1,000 was a bank loan! Restoration started in the early 1980s and proceeded as fast as fund raising permitted. The group involved with *Sir Archibald Sinclair* had the benefit of some sponsorship, but the bulk of the money was raised through the Bluebell Railway Battle of Britain Locomotive Group 300 Club and a sales stand at Sheffield Park station: it is estimated that around £350,000 was eventually spent on the restoration. Naturally, there were setbacks on the way and many problems had to be resolved, but the biggest one was undoubtedly manufacturing a new tender. A Bulleid tender frame was acquired from a South Wales steelworks but was found to be distorted and, after the removal of all useable components, the frame was discarded, so a new tender had to built almost from scratch. The boiler was steam tested in June 2008 and the almost completed locomotive made a number of test runs in early 2009 before its official launch. One can only imagine the sense of fulfilment and satisfaction experienced by those involved in bringing a decaying hulk back to life. *Mike Esau*

Back when there was a very long way to go! Red oxide protective paint has been applied to parts of its boiler barrel, but otherwise No.34059 looks decidedly forlorn as it sits in the Pump House siding at Sheffield Park on 6th July 1980. Part of *Camelot* is just visible on the left of the shot. *David Cox*

The year 2009 was noteworthy for a very cold snap in mid-December which severely dislocated most forms of transport. Unfortunately the Bluebell was not immune and the weather played havoc with the Christmas train timetable on 19th/20th December, some services having to be cancelled entirely due to problems with frozen points and suchlike. Here, the Maunsell Society's hard-working 'Mogul' No.1638, emitting an absolutely magnificent smoke effect, climbs Freshfield bank with the delayed 11.36am 'Santa Special' from Sheffield Park to Kingscote. A memorable end to a glorious fifty years. *Jon Bowers*